Malawi: A Turning Point

To Bridie

With gratitude for all your support

Fr. Trevor Cullen.
May 22 1994

Trevor Cullen was born on 19 July 1957 in Hackney, East London. He belongs to a religious order, the Montfort Missionaries, and studied for the priesthood at the Missionary Institute, London. His degrees include an S.T.B. (Theology) and M.A. (Religious Studies) from Leuven University, Belgium, and an M.A. in International Journalism from City University, London. After ordination, he worked in Malawi from 1981 to 1991, first in a rural parish and then as a youth chaplain and lecturer in Theology. Presently he is Rector of Montfort House, Hendon. In September 1994 he begins an internship at Vatican Radio.

Malawi:
A Turning Point

Trevor Cullen

The Pentland Press
Edinburgh – Cambridge – Durham

© Trevor Cullen, 1994

First published in 1994 by
The Pentland Press Ltd
1 Hutton Close
South Church
Bishop Auckland
Durham

All rights reserved.
Unauthorised duplication
contravenes existing laws.

ISBN 1-85821-186-7

Typeset by Carnegie Publishing, 18 Maynard St., Preston
Printed and bound by Antony Rowe Ltd., Chippenham

To
the friendly, warm-hearted Malawian people
who deserve better from their leaders

Table of Contents

	Preamble	1
	Introduction	5
Chapter 1	Background Information	9
Chapter 2	Early Signs of Dissent	29
Chapter 3	The Bishops' Letter	34
Chapter 4	Formation of Opposition Groups	53
Chapter 5	Factory Strikes	59
Chapter 6	Western Donors Cut Aid	62
Chapter 7	The Role of the Christian Churches	65
Chapter 8	The Referendum Process	70
Chapter 9	A Changed Climate	81
Chapter 10	An Evaluation of the Bishops' Letter	86
Chapter 11	An Uncertain Future	92
	Endnotes	103
	Bibliography	115
Pastoral Letter	The Catholic Bishops speak out	120

Preamble

Journalist Adewale Maja-Pearce described what happened one day when he tried to walk through the main street of Blantyre, Malawi's commercial capital:

> It happened that I was in Blantyre on the day that President Banda was expected back from Harare (20 October 1991). The city itself was closed from mid-day onwards but it wasn't until six o'clock that evening, four hours after his plane had touched down, that his entourage made its way slowly through the crowded streets to the presidential palace.
>
> The entourage consisted of 10 police cars and four motorcycle outriders. They were followed less than a minute later by a blue Rolls Royce. I strained hard to catch a glimpse of Banda. All I saw was a frail hand waving a fly whisk.
>
> There was another short interval and then I began to count the number of army and police vehicles bringing up the rear. I stopped at 40.
>
> What interested me more than this all too obvious display of naked authority was the behaviour of the crowd. There was no clapping or cheering. The people who lined up on either side of the main road stood silently in fading light, and it was the silence of people stunned into submission by what journalist Julie Flint had called "the totalitarian, highly personalised regime that is living proof that repression can work".
>
> (*Index on Censorship,* April 1992, page 14).

Richard Dowden, *The Independent*'s Africa editor, visited Malawi 20 months later. He stood on the same Blantyre street and wrote:

Convoys of cars and lorries flying yellow tags, the colour of the multi-party groups, paraded through the main street, their occupants hanging out of the windows, giving the two-finger victory salute.

Gangs of young people were shouting, waving, chanting "No more Banda" and other slogans against the man and the party that have made Malawi a totalitarian state for the past 29 years. "This is our second liberation," said one man."

What events led to such a transformation? *Malawi: A Turning Point* tries to pinpoint the Catholic bishops' pastoral letter, *Living Our Faith:* (8 March 1992), as the turning point and catalyst in Malawi's struggle for democracy.

Political change is influenced by a combination of factors, often complex ones, and it is too simplistic to state that one public letter forced the government to abandon nearly 30 years of absolute control. Yet, interviews with more than 40 people (mainly Malawians), suggest the bishop's letter acted as a decisive breakthrough in dismantling Banda's dictatorship.

Malawi: A Turning Point examines the context, content and consequences of the bishops' letter. Numerous references, several fact sheets and a diary of events provide important background information for understanding recent events in Malawi, especially preparations for Malawi's first multi-party election due to be held on 17 May.

The book follows a chronological order. Chapters 1 and 2 provide background information in order to understand why the letter was written; chapter 3 details the build-up, content and reaction to the letter; chapters 4-6 show direct links between the bishops' letter and the political, economic and social developments in Malawi after March 1992. The remaining chapters discuss the role of the Christian churches, the referendum process and Malawi's uncertain future.

My interest in the topic stems from the ten enjoyable years I spent working in Malawi (1981–91), first in rural parish work and then as youth chaplain in Zomba and a teacher in Balaka. This book is a continuation of my service to the Malawian people.

Trevor Cullen
1 May 1994

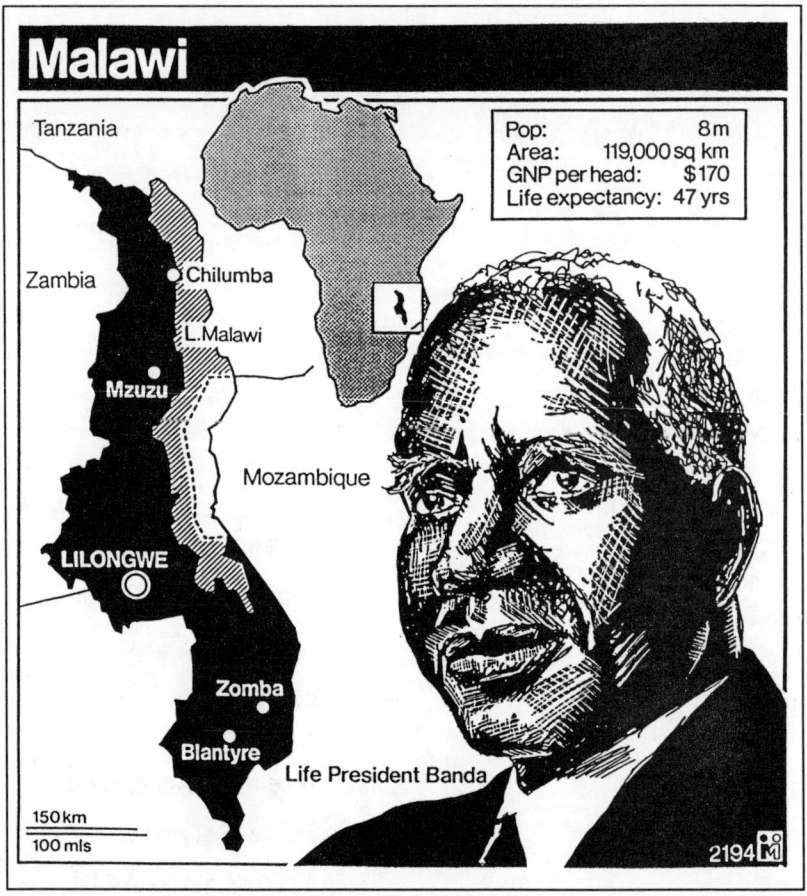

Introduction

Sunday Mass in Malawi on 8 March 1992, began in the usual way. By the time it ended Malawi was never going to be the same again.

During the Mass a Lenten pastoral letter written by the country's seven Catholic bishops was read out in all churches.

This was no ordinary letter. Entitled *Living Our Faith*, it contained the first public internal condemnation of the government's human rights record since independence in 1964.

More than 16,000 copies of the letter were printed and read in all 130 catholic parishes throughout Malawi. Since each Catholic parish has several smaller churches attached to the main church, it is possible the letter was read out in more than 1,000 churches throughout the country.

Parishioners listened in amazement as the bishops accused the ruling Malawi Congress Party (MCP) of gross human rights abuses in health care and education and of interfering with the judiciary. Detention

> **'Revealing some evils of our society is seen as slandering the country; some people have paid dearly for their political opinions'**
> *— From the Bishops' Pastoral Letter*

without trial, the gap between the rich and poor and increasing government corruption were included on the list of allegations.

In a country where prisons and graveyards were full of those who dared to criticise Banda's 29-year dictatorial rule, the bishops' decision to speak out involved serious risk to their own lives.

The bishops survived and their letter acted as a bombshell that exploded the myth of Banda having total control over every aspect of Malawian life.

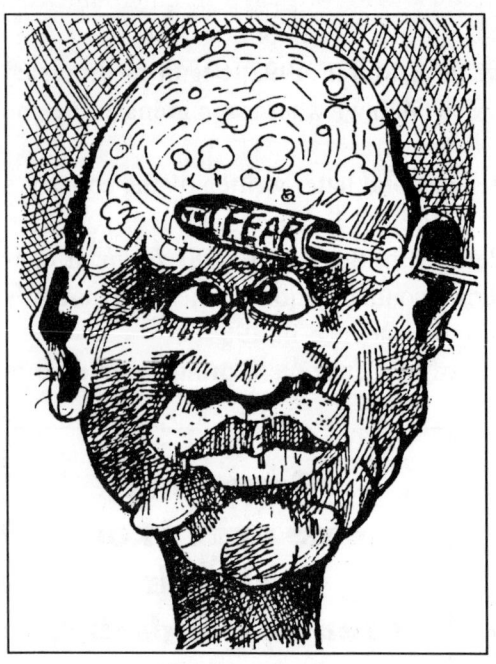

The government responded swiftly and declared the pastoral letter to be a seditious document and possession of it became a criminal offence.

During an emergency meeting of senior officials of the ruling Malawi Congress Party (MCP) in Lilongwe on 11 March, some participants called for the bishops to be killed. In a speech the previous month Banda had warned exiled government opponents that they would be used as "meat for the crocodiles".

Government anger intensified. An editorial in the government-run *Malawi News* (14–20 March) described the authors of the letter as "Mafia-style crooks aiming to import IRA terrorism into this country".

Meanwhile, public support sided with the bishops. The following Sunday (15 March) saw Catholic churches packed with Catholics and non-Catholics, while students from Zomba University and Blantyre Polytechnic launched unprecedented public demonstrations in support of the bishops, forcing the government to close both institutions.

Such events had never happened before in Malawi's short history. Further confrontations seemed inevitable.

Several questions arose. Why had the bishops waited nearly 30 years to speak out? Would the letter represent a turning point? Or, was it merely a catalyst for further developments?

To appreciate the content and impact of the letter, it is necessary to examine certain political developments since independence.

Malawi

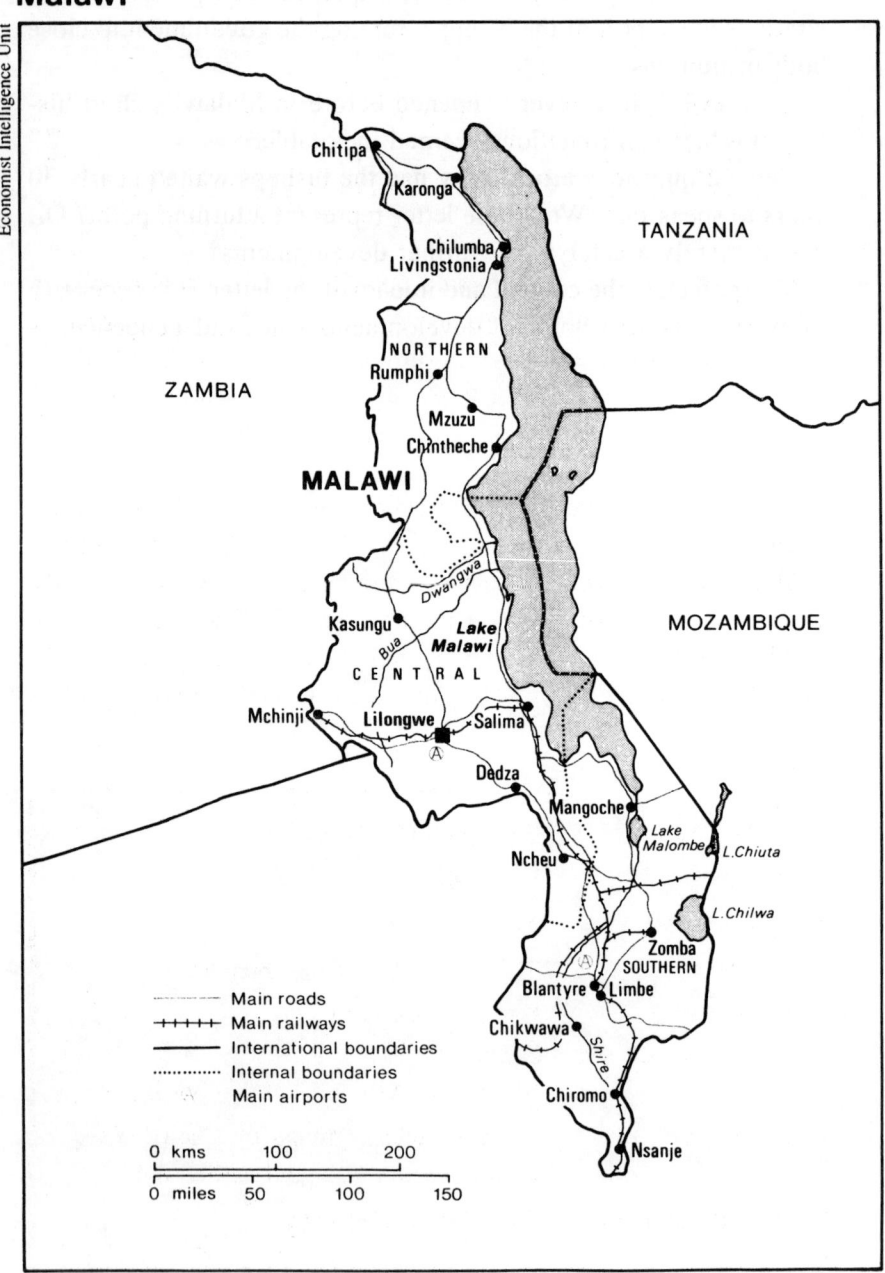

Chapter 1

Background Information

Malawi is a small landlocked country, bordering Tanzania in the north, Zambia in the west and Mozambique to the east and south. More than eight million people live in an area half the size of Britain. The country is dominated by Lake Malawi – Africa's third largest lake – which runs the whole length of the country.

Malawi is designated by the United Nations as a Least Developed Country with a per capita Gross National Product (GNP) of $170, an infant mortality rate of 143 per 1000 live births, a life expectancy of 47 years and a literacy rate of 47 per cent.[2]

More than 80% of people work in agriculture compared to 15% in services and 3% in industry. In 1993, agricultural commodities

Official Name:	Republic of Malawi
Population:	8,428,000
Area:	118,480 sq. km.
Capital:	Lilongwe (220,000 inhabitants)
Other Cities:	Blantyre (402,000)
	Zomba (53,000)
	Mzuzu (87,000)
The People:	The main ethnic groups are Chewa, Yao, Tonga, Tumbuka, Ngoni and Nyanja.
Official Languages:	English and Chechewa.[1]

accounted for 93.6% of Malawi's domestic exports. Tobacco is the largest export crop (75%) followed by sugar (9%), tea (7%), cotton (2.5%) and coffee (2%).[3]

1.2 Banda's Rise to Power

Malawi was formerly the British protectorate of Nyasaland (1890). In 1944, the first national political organisation, the Nyasaland African Congress (NAC) was formed. Banda, working as a general practitioner in North London, was an active NAC supporter

	Important Dates
1500	Maravi people migrated from (Zaire) into Malawi.
1859	David Livingstone visited Lake Nyasa.
1875	Free Church of Scotland establish Livingstone Mission.
1891	British Protectorate declared over the 'Nyasaland districts'. Renamed Nyasaland Protectorate in 1907.
1944	The Nyasaland African Congress (NAC) formed.
1953	Federation of Rhodesia and Nyasaland.
1958	Banda elected leader of the Malawi Congress Party (MCP).
1959–60	Banda imprisoned with 1,000 MCP supporters.
1963–66	Banda becomes Prime Minister.
1964	Independence (6 July).
1966	Malawi becomes a Republic within the Commonwealth. Banda elected President (6 July).
1971	Banda made Life President.
1993	Referendum win for pro-democracy supporters (14 June). Constitution changed to allow opposition parties (28 June).

	Banda's Background
Birth:	14 May 1906 (official)
Education:	AME Wilberforce Institute (1925)
	University of Chicago (1930)
	Meharry Medical School (1932)
	Royal College of Physicians and Surgeons, Edinburgh (1938)
Medical practice:	Liverpool 1939; North Shields 1940–4; Willesden, North London 1946–5; Ghana 1953–57
Qualifications:	M.D., L.R.C.S., L.R.F.P., Ph.B., Hon.DSc., Hon.LL.D (Massachussetts), Hon.LL.D (Indiana), Hon. DSc. (Meharry), Hon.LL.D., (Malawi), F.R.C.S., F.R.C.P.(Edinburgh)
Political positions:	1958 Elected leader of the MCP
	1963–66 Prime Minister
	1966 President
	1971 Life President
Official Title:	His Excellency, Life President Ngwazi Dr Hastings Kamuzu Banda.

especially after 1953 when Nyasaland was linked with two other dependencies, Northern and Southern Rhodesia (now Zambia and Zimbabwe), to form the Federation of Rhodesia and Nyasaland.

NAC feared the Federation would mean domination by white Rhodesian settlers and actively opposed it. In 1957 the young leaders of NAC invited Banda to Nyasaland to assume the leadership of NAC.

Banda's outspoken attacks against the Colonial Office and the Nyasaland government, his generous financial support for NAC and the hospitality he extended to NAC members visiting London had impressed NAC officials. They reasoned that Banda's age and experience would help in leading the country to independence.

Banda returned to Malawi from Ghana in July 1958 leaving behind Mrs French, the woman he lived with in Britain and Ghana, and their son David. His medical career was at an end in London and Ghana. Aged 60, it seemed unlikely he could revive it. Malawi offered an escape and a future.[4]

Elected as party leader at the NAC conference in August 1958, Banda was allowed to appoint officers of the congress and members of the executive council. The NAC leadership hoped Banda would confine himself to a symbolic role while they wielded real power. They made a costly mistake in giving Banda too much power at such an early stage.

Since Banda was unknown to most Malawians, the NAC organised an intensive publicity drive. Hailed as "the greatest of Nyasaland's sons" and "the equal of any European", Banda's popularity soared to the level of hero worship. The campaign's success resulted in "the young militants having not merely a leader but a messiah, and it was soon to become apparent that Dr Banda, intoxicated by the adulation, was delighted to be cast in that role".[5]

In early 1959 NAC launched a campaign of non-violent civil disobedience. Within weeks NAC was banned and 1500 supporters, including Banda, were detained under emergency powers. They were held for one year in southern Rhodesia.

Britain began to accept the inevitability of Nyasaland's independence. In September 1959 the Malawi Congress party (MCP) was formed to replace the banned NAC. Elections in August 1961 gave the MCP a majority of seats in the Legislative Council. Self-government, with Banda as Prime Minister, followed in 1963.

By then definite signs of Banda's dictatorial style had begun to emerge. Speaking in the Legislative assembly in June 1962, he declared: "There is no dispute in our party. We don't say what do you want, what is it? It is what Kamuzu says that goes."[6]

Banda's determination to hold on to power and reject any form of dissent was re-echoed in a later speech at a political rally in Blantyre in May 1964. "... This kind of thing where the leader says this but somebody else says that: now who is the leader? That is not the Malawi system. The Malawi system, the Malawi style is that Kamuzu says it's just that, and then it's finished."[7]

A former cabinet minister remarked: "Whenever you criticised him (Banda), he flared up so violently that you had to consider your own position. You did not want to be dismissed from the central committee of the party or from the cabinet."[8]

Dunduza Chisiza, a prominent young economist and potentially Banda's main rival for leadership, did challenge Banda's economic policies. He died in 1962 at the age of 32 from injuries sustained in a mysterious car accident. The incident raised further fears about disagreeing with Banda's policies. More "accidents" were to follow prompting the remark that "careless driving appears all too common among Malawi's politicans."[9]

1.3 Political Conflict

Only two months after independence in July 1964, Banda dismissed four cabinet ministers for disagreeing with his foreign policy towards South Africa and Portugal and his recognition of the People's Republic of China. The ministers included Kanyama Chiume, Orton Chirwa, Augustine Bwanausi and Rose Chibambo. Three other ministers resigned in protest and were forced into exile in Zambia.

What is now termed the 'Cabinet crisis' was to prove a decisive event in Malawi's post-independence history. It exposed Banda's tendency towards authoritarian rule and created an exiled opposition movement.

Foreign policy was not the only contentious issue. The ministers questioned Banda's preference for a slower rate of africanisation and his acceptance of the Skinner report which gave Malawians lower wages for doing the same work as Europeans. They felt Banda treated the government as his own personal estate and accused him of favouring certain politicians such as John Tembo and Aleke Banda. Banda frequently belittled and irritated his ministers by calling them "His Boys".

The crisis came too soon after independence and minisiters acted too hastilty in trying to remove Banda. It only served to consolidate Banda's power base and he continued to create a climate of fear with threatening statements against his opponents: "These people are wild animals. They must be destroyed. No beating about the bush. Arrest them, but if they resist arrest, well anything you do is alright as far as I am concerned."[10] Such outbursts killed off any effective opposition.

This led to the rise of 'the family', namely Mama Kadzamira, Malawi's official hostess, and her uncle, the Hon John Tembo, the current Minister of State.

It was not until 1983 that government ministers spoke out again. Banda wanted to spend a period of time abroad, which set off a constitutional crisis. A faction, led by Mama Kadzamira, wanted Mr Tembo to be the 'caretaker' president.

This was challenged by three leading cabinet ministers, Aaron Gadama, Minister for the Central Region and Leader of the House, Twaibu Sangala, Minister for Health, Dick Matenje, Secretary General of the MCP, and David Chiwanga, MP for Chikwawa. This time Banda's methods of control were well established. According to government reports, they were killed in a 'car crash' on their way home from a cabinet meeting.

The local police who arrived at the scene of the accident discovered fresh bullet wounds in each of the corpses and were told in a directive from police headquarters in Blantyre to put the bodies in sealed coffins and refrain from talking to the press. At the four different burials, villagers were ordered not to open the coffins.

Describing the murder of the ministers, Amnesty International's report, *Where Silence Rules: The Suppression of Dissent in Malawi*

(October 1990), concludes: "Any hope of serious reform died with them."

Banda abandoned his medical sabbatical but the Tembo/Kadzamira faction continued to consolidate its wealth, power and influence, wielding all three effectively against any opposition.

Mr Tembo's influence throughout the 1980s was such that as Minister without Portfolio he was able to control the MCP. Cabinet ministers sought his permission before taking decisions. As chairman of 24 major companies within Malawi, Mr Tembo also had the support of the business community. It came as no surprise when Banda appointed him Minister of State in 1991.[11]

Chitukuko Cha Amai M'Malawi (CCAM) – Women in Development – was founded ostensibly to promote the role of women and charitable activities. In reality it served to cement Mama Kadzamira's influential political role and unsurprisingly she was elected its first and only national advisor. All women became automatic members.

Banda continued to finesse the patronage system. He rewarded key figures in the society; the army, police, civil servants, and large estate owners. They became part of the status quo with a vested interest in the survival of the state and Banda.

Shifting ministers between portfolios with amazing regularity prevented them from gaining institutional power bases and acted as a control device. Real executive power lay with senior civil servants who were hand-picked by Banda.

Malawian critics living abroad were sought out and often silenced. Attati Mpakati, leader of the exiled Socialist League of Malawi (LESOMA), had eight of his fingers blown off by a parcel bomb in Maputo, Mozambique, in 1979. Banda stated publicly that "his boys" were responsible for the attack. In March 1983 Mr Mpakati was found murdered in a storm drain in Harare. Two Malawians were arrested but later released for lack of evidence.

Mkwapatira Mhango, a journalist exiled to Zambia for criticising Banda's autocratic style, died after a fire-bomb attack on his

Lusaka home on 13 October 1989. Ten people died including Mhango's two wives and young children.

Patronage, repression and a totalitarian hold on all aspects of life made it impossible to organise political opposition within Malawi up until March 1992.

1.4 Other Methods of Repression

The Preventive Detention Bill (1964) and the Public Safety Regulations Act (1965) provided the legal framework for arrest and detention. Mass detentions followed with more than 1,000 opposition supporters being imprisoned without trial. Most remained in detention for more than 10 years.

The extensive use of detention without trial of nationalist supporters by the colonial authorities between 1959–61 provided an administrative model for the new government.

Richard Carver monitored political developments in Malawi for Amnesty International from 1984–92. "In the 1960s and 1970s hundreds were detained," said Mr Carver. "The authorities were not obliged to publish names and numbers, and detention powers were completely arbitrary."[12]

The detention of Jack Mapanje, the country's leading poet and former head of English at Zomba university, is a typical example of how detention worked in Malawi. He was detained in September 1987 and imprisoned for three-and-half years. He was never told the reason for his arrest.

"Dictatorships never tell their victims why you are arrested or released," complains Mr Mapanje. "I kept thinking of Banda's words that rebels would rot, rot and rot."

"I felt very bitter for the first few months. I was a respected member of the community. For 22 months I was not allowed a visit from my wife or children, not even a visit from a friend. In prison I met people who had been there for a longer period and so we developed strategies for survival. We said that if we die here the system wins."

Mr Mapanje explained why intellectuals were detained. "President Banda feared those who had different views. So he established an extremely draconian system; he killed creatively. His supporters brutalised the ordinary people in the villages as well as those who were educated. He became a god-like figure, effectively unapproachable. Anyone who was educated and an independent thinker was usually referred to as a 'rebel' – and any sort of disagreement, even if it was constructive criticism was not accepted."

Banda insisted on total control: "If, to maintain stability and efficient administration I have to detain 10,000, 100,000, I will do it."[13]

In February 1989 Banda ordered all northern teachers in the south and central regions to return to their home districts because of alleged nepotism towards northern students. The education system was thrown into confusion with a severe shortage of trained teachers in the south and too many in the north. Despite feelings of anger and resentment the teachers obeyed without any display of public protest. Their outward sign of obedience masked a deeper reality: fear of prison and possible torture kept them silent.

A vigorous personality cult operated throughout the country and Banda was always referred to by his full set of titles. Everything he did was slavishly reported on the front pages of the newspapers or became headline news on the radio.

Important institutions are named after him – Kamuzu International Airport, Kamuzu Stadium, Kamuzu Bridge, Kamuzu Academy, Kamuzu Highway, and Kamuzu Central Hospital.

By 1986 Banda had turned the MCP Women's League into "Kamuzu's Mbumba" reducing their role to that of dancers and "praise singers" during ceremonial occasions. The CCAM cornered the support of those women not among the Mbumba entourage.

The activities of CCAM and the mbumba affected family life. The husband and wife were not free to discuss politics in case an unguarded remark was relayed to the party; money had to be set aside for buying the official dress – a large wrap-around cloth illustrated with several pictures of a younger looking Banda; obligatory outings to far-off party rallies and compulsory work on communal farms to raise funds for CCAM left children unsupervised and neglected. As a result mistrust among family members grew while Banda's control seemed total.

1.5 Censorship

Banda controlled the flow of information in order to bolster his political dominance. The 1968 Censorship and Control of Entertainment Bill made it an offence – punishable by five years' imprisonment – "to publish anything likely to undermine the authority of, or public confidence in, the government."

The scope of the Bill removed any loopholes found in previous regulations in regard to freedom of speech.

The Bill regulated and controlled the making and exhibition of cinema pictures, the importation, production, dissemination and possession of undesirable publications, pictures and records. The Malawi Censorship Board (MCB) was set up to implement the Bill and by 1975, the MCB had banned 849 books, 100 periodicals and 16 films.

Some publications slipped through the control net. The MCB banned one particular book and unknowingly Banda recommended his cabinet to read it after he brought it back from Meharry College, Tennessee. When Prince Charles visited Malawi in 1987, he was unaware of the MCB list of banned films and encouraged his hosts to see *Room with a View*.[14]

The performance or presentation of stage plays and public entertainments were also monitored. The banning of Simon and Garfunkel's song 'Cecilia' because it happened to be the first name of Banda's offical hostess, showed the extensive scope and arbitrary nature of of the Bill.

Background Information

The two main newspapers *The Daily Times* and *Malawi News* were owned by Banda's own Press Holdings conglomerate. The only radio station, Malawi Broadcasting Corporation (MBC), was government-run. One human rights report summed up the role of the media in Malawi as "primarily to catalogue the Chief of State's words and activities."[15]

Foreign publications were vetted minutely for anything that might be critical of any aspect of political, social or economic life.

Due to the expulsion of all foreign journalists and the detention of any local ones who reported – often inadvertently – about the country, Malawians were unable to find out what was happening in their own country unless they tuned into the BBC World Service.

Mike Hall worked for 18 months as the BBC World Service correspondent in Malawi. "I was based in Blantyre, the first correspondent since Philip Short in the 1960s. In February 1990, I was told to leave the country or I would be deported which was tantamount to the same thing. I was never told the reasons and had only 48 hours to pack my belongings."

"Operating in Malawi was extremely difficult," said Mr Hall. "I had no access to cabinet ministers and little rapport with local journalists because they could get life imprisonment for passing on information. Diplomats and aid workers were my main sources."

Talented Malawian writers such as Lupenga Phande, Felix Mnthali, and Frank Chipasula left the country. Those that stayed invented subtle metaphors. "Dawn" or "cockerel" referred to the MCP while "Chingwe's hole" was a veiled reference to detention centres. The phrase "The leopards of Dedza" was used when describing Mr Tembo or Mama Kadzamira.

An independent fortnightly business newspaper *The Financial Post* appeared in 1991. Read mainly by expatriates, it adopted a non-partisan tone and prepared the way for a rush of newspapers in early 1993.

1.6 Paramilitary Activities

Detention without trial and tight press control was combined with ruthless political control at the grass roots. The Malawi Young Pioneers (MYP) – founded as a youth organisation to carry out agricultural tasks – split into two groups when Banda created the military wing of the MYP to monitor any disloyalty against him and the MCP.

In 1965 the Young Pioneers Act gave them the power of arrest and freed them from any police action. They functioned as a combination of political militia and intelligence network.

Banda told parliament: "The young pioneers cannot be arrested by any policeman without my consent. If a young pioneer arrests anybody and brings them to the police station, the police officer in charge of that station must not release them. If he does he is committing a crime."[16]

Trained by Israeli intelligence officers, the MYP worked closely with the Malawi Police (MP) and their influence, especially in the rural areas, was immense. *Index on Censorship* reported how the young pioneers were employed "to arrest, interrogate and detain anyone for information thought to be detrimental to the government. They pick up people at night, ransack their houses and the unfortunate are detained and ill-treated."[17]

Henry Chimango, chairman of the Washington-based human rights group, Malawi Action Committee (MAC) described the pioneers as "hand-picked thugs of the MCP. They acted as the eyes and the ears of a highly repressive state. Somebody in a bar talking about the need for multi-party democracy often ended up in a jail two days later."

It was usual for a squad of young pioneers, dressed in their distinctive red and green shirts, to turn up at busy market towns and rural centres on the main market days and lock people inside the walled markets until they produced or paid for an MCP party card. The government, under pressure from donor countries, abandoned this practice in January 1993.

Despite the MYP repressive tactics, it was the Malawi Police Mobil Force (MPMF) who hunted down political suspects and imprisoned them without trial. A secret police force, The Special Branch, sought out dissidents abroad and were linked to political assassinations as in the case of Attati Mpakati in Harare in 1983.[18]

1.7 The Economy

Six years of pre-independence instability (1958–64) prevented any real economic growth. But economic optimists predicted that "the perilously weak ecomony Dr Banda inherited could hardly fail to improve on its 1964 performance".[19]

A noticeable economic upswing occurred between 1965–1975 with an impressive set of improvements. By 1978, The Malawi GNP was more than twice its 1964 figure: from $88 to $190; government expenditure on development had increased by 25 times the 1964 allocation.

Even staunch critics recognised the extent of Banda's early achievements. "Malawi's growth had been satisfactory especially for a country that at its independence was given little chance of success. Underlying the success was a considerable mobilisation of internal funds for investment, especially through the fiscal system; an active and successful search for foreign grants and loans and relatively effective use of investment funds, at least until the end of the '70s."[20]

Banda, firmly at the helm of economic policy, frequently reminded his audiences that he masterminded the revival. "A leader who depends on others, even his own officials or outside experts, is a prisoner. And I never want to be a prisoner on any subject, not one. I accept advice from so called experts, so called advisors, so called specialists only when their advice agrees with my own ideas and not at any other time."[21]

If he had died or retired around 1975, political opponents and economists would have assessed his autocratic rule in a more positive way.

By 1979 financial and economic indicators had begun to worry policy makers.[22]

The economic downturn led to the adoption of an International Monetary Fund (IMF) adjustment programme. Initially, the results were encouraging with a drop in inflation, a deficit in the balance of payments and an increase in investments. By 1988 a four-year IMF Enhanced Structural Adjustment Facility (ESAF) had to be negotiated.[23]

Inflation rose substantially in the mid-1980s. Civil war in Mozambique blocked Malawi's access to the port at Beira. Instead imported goods were redirected through a series of other countries including South Africa, Botswana, Zimbabawe, Zambia and eventually into Malawi. This added an extra £38 million to the annual transport bill and forced several increases in domestic prices. There was no corresponding wage increase.[24]

Large private coffee and tea estates and the enormous expense of financing Banda's extensive patronage system, drained the economy of vital foreign currency. Banda's 'private' expenses and

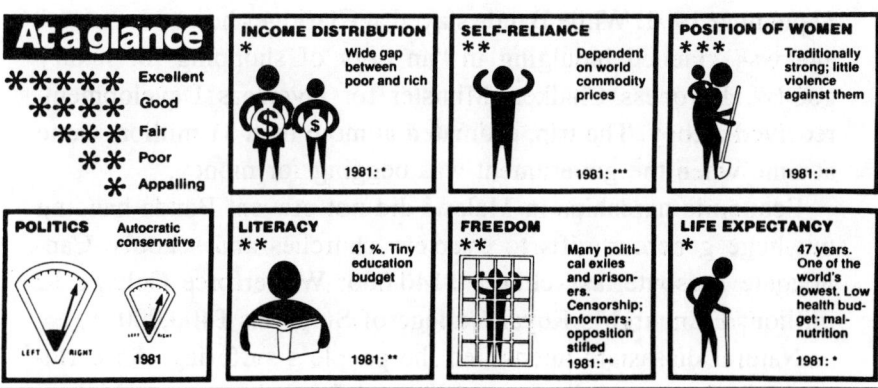

Per capita GNP:	$170 (1989)
Annual growth:	0.6% (1980–88)
Annual inflation:	1965–80: 7.4% 1980–91: 14.9%
Imports:	$505 million (1980)
Exports:	$267 million (1989)
Major markets:	EC: 40% Africa 16%
	USA and Canada 14% Japan 9%
External debt:	$1.4 billion (1989)
Debt service:	28% of exports (1989)
Development aid received	$394 million (1989): 24.9% of GNP

Third World Guide, 1993/4

political rallies were often paid for by siphoning off funds from Banda's Press Holdings companies and a false economy arose when these companies began to fund large unsecured loans to Banda.[25]

The ABC programme *Prime Time Live* exposed the extent of government extravangance when Banda travelled to London in September 1991. While Banda stayed at Claridges hotel, his entourage was videoed indulging in "an orgy of shopping for luxury goods". Baroness Chalker, Minister for Overseas Development, received a copy. The trip, estimated at more than $1 million, came at time when the government was begging for money.

Economic hardships in Malawi did not prevent Banda handing out huge generous gifts to overseas churches and schools; Cannongate Presbyteriasn church £140,000; Wilberforce College $2 million: Edinburgh's Royal College of Surgeons £400,000.[26]

Natural diasasters intensified the people's suffering. An earthquake in the central district in 1990 and floods in southern Malawi the following year exacerbated food shortages caused by the influx of more than 1 million refugees fleeing the civil war in neighbouring Mozambique. A severe drought in early 1992 led to widespread hunger in the centre and south of the country.[27]

Deteriorating economic conditions in the rural areas – where 88% of people live – and rampant government corruption contributed to a greater readiness to associate with the content of the bishops' letter.

Other facts

Infant mortality:	143 per 1000 in the first year
	195 per 1000 in the first five years
people per hospital:	15,630
people per doctor:	33,347
people per dentist:	582,467
people per pharmacist:	728,083
people per nurse:	6,080

Figures for 1989, *World Development Report*, 1993

1.8 The Catholic Church

Two Catholic religious orders – the White Fathers and the Montfort Missionaries – came to Malawi in 1903, 28 years after the Scottish Free Church set up its first mission at Livingstonia in 1875.

The Catholics and Presbyterians differed in their missionary approach. Catholicism took root in the villages with the building of churches, primary schools and rural clinics. The Presbyterians concentrated on educating Malawians to become teachers, artisans and evangelists.

The Chilembwe rising of 1915 exposed the difference between

the two churches. Among the rebels were 84 baptised members of the Presbyterian church but no Catholics. While the Presbyterian missions were regarded with intense suspicion by the colonial government, the Catholic missionaries gained new prestige as staunch upholders of the status quo.[28]

During the 1940s and 1950s, when the MCP began to dominate Malawian politics, the Catholics were identified with the wrong side. This was confirmed in 1961 when the Right Rev John Theunissen, Bishop of Blantyre, backed the Christian Democratic Party (CDP), while most Malawians supported the MCP.

In contrast, it is estimated that of the 1,500 'hard core' MCP members placed in detention camps during the state of emergency in 1959, more than 1,200 were Presbyterians. Greater commitment to the liberation struggle enabled the CCAP church to become the dominant religious force in Malawi after 1964.[29]

Religious adherence

Christians:	65% (Catholics 22%)
	Catholic population 1,893,000
Moslems:	16%
Other faiths	19% [30]

Banda's attitude towards the Catholic church – as with all the churches – was to retrict its role to 'partnership in development'. "In some countries the Church and State tend to be open enemies... Thank God this is not the case in Malawi ... Church and State are partners in looking after the children of God on earth."[31]

Besides, the government needed the services of the church. The extensive network of church schools, hospitals and clinics, revealed the extensive influence of the churches. A report by the Christian

Church Schools		Students
Primary:	926	412,468
Secondary	41	10,331
State Schools		
Primary:	2,660	1,066,642
Secondary:	91	30,030
Mission hospitals:	19	
Orphanages:	7	
Handicapped:	3	
Dispensaries:	61	
Nurseries:	10	
Welfare centres:	39	

Statistical Yearbook of the Church, Vatican Press, July 1993

Health Association of Malawi (CHAM) estimated that the churches provide "over 30 per cent all health care facilities in the country" and train "about 85 per cent of enrolled nurses and midwives in Malawi. This cadre is the backbone of health delivery in the country."[32]

Banda vigorously supressed any form of church protest. When the Jehovah's Witnesses refused to buy the MCP party card, 21,000 members fled to Zambia in November 1973 to avoid persecution and torture. Within a month Zambia repatriated 17,000 members. Up to 15,000 then fled to Mozambique only to be expelled two years later. By January 1976, 5,000 had been arrested by the police. They were freed from prison in 1977.[33]

Tension between the MCP and the Catholic church reached a peak in 1982. The Most Rev James Chiona, Archbishop of Blantyre, challenged the government by stating in a Sunday homily that parishioners in his area were suffering from serious food shortages due to the severe drought.

The next day he was questioned by police and MCP officials. They banned him from representing the church at official MCP functions.

Constant fear of retaliation prevented a concerted attack by church leaders on the government. For example, one of the Catholic bishops, who was too frightened to give his name, openly admits that in 1983, when three ministers died in a car crash, he knew they had been murdered: "I know a priest who saw it happen. The car was pushed down the side of the bridge to give the impression of an accident. But they were shot before that."

Asked why he remained silent, he said: "The European missionaries could have said something and been deported. But me, I'd be taken away and I was too frightened."

The Malawian bishops broke their silence on 8 March 1992. It came as a shock to the government. Only four days before, the bishops had visited Banda at Sanjika palace in Blantyre to present Mgr Tarcisius Ziyayc as the new Bishop of Dedza. Front page headlines in *The Daily Times* proclaimed 'Church and State in Partnership.' Within days, the alleged friendship was in tatters.

Chapter 2

Early Signs of Dissent

The murder of three cabinet ministers and a member of parliament in May 1983, signalled the end of any immediate reforms.[1]

However, exiled opposition groups continued to protest against Banda's dicatorship. The Socialist League of Malawi (LESOMA) led by Dr Atati Mpakati in Mozambique, and the Malawi Freedom Movement (MAFREMO) based in Tanzania under the leadership of Orton Chirwa wanted "to restore democracy, justice and liberty to Malawi".

Disunity and effective penetration by the intelligence services limited the impact of the opposition groups. The Special Branch spared no mercy in dealing with outspoken exiles.

The kidnap and sentencing to death of two prominent Malawian lawyers, Orton Chirwa and his wife Vera in December 1981, evoked an international outcry. Due to their persistent criticism of the government, Banda had them tried for treason in a rigged trial at one of Blantyre's traditional courts. Under intense international pressure for staging such "a mockery of justice", Banda commuted their death sentences to life-imprisonment.

In 1992, a year before Mr Chirwa's suspicious death in Zomba prison, the authorities claimed they had intercepted some of his smuggled letters. Amnesty International's report *Malawi: Prison conditions, cruel punishment and detention without trial*, February 1992, revealed the severity of the punishment meted out to the 72-year-old prisoner: "He was kept in a squatting position in handcuffs and leg-irons, which were chained to an iron bar behind his knees. He remained in that position for two days with no lavatory or other sanitary facilities."

Talking in the House of Commons on 11 May 1993, Mrs Chirwa expanded on her husband's treatment. "We met for the only time after nearly 10 years in the same prison ... Orton said they tortured him terribly. Often they tied his hands and feet to a stone pole. Very frequently they transferred him to the execution cell ... He was found dead in his cell but I never saw a report of how he died. No inquest was ever held."

Protests by Mkwapatira Mhango, a journalist exiled in Zambia, led to his death in a fire-bomb attack on his Lusaka home on 13 October 1989. Altogether 10 people died including Mhango's two wives and seven young children. The government denied any involvement saying it was the result of internal feuding among Malawian exiles.

Banda had attacked Mr Mhango by name in a speech three weeks earlier and the presence of Malawian security squads in Lusaka was common knowledge among Malawian refugees living in Zambia.[2]

Even mild criticism was outlawed. In October 1989, *Chirunga Newsletter*, a magazine produced by students at Zomba University, criticised a decision not to re-admit students who had interrupted their studies for maternity leave. Hardly sensational criticism but in a Malawian context it seemed a daring move. Yet the editor and two reporters were suspended for the rest of the academic year while four other students were expelled and prevented from getting jobs.[3]

Two days later the suspensions produced the first ever student demonstrations. A peaceful march of some 600 university students converged on the police headquarters in Zomba. The students dispersed leaving behind a visible sign of popular dissatisfaction with the government.

Government ruthlessness was again displayed in an incident – never reported in the Malawi press – when police shot dead more than 20 protestors in Lilongwe on 18 March 1991.

The protestors were angry with police treatment of a businessman who had beaten one of his employees to death for alleged theft. Angry local people threw stones at the police because they thought the businessman had bribed them. The police opened fire killing many innocent passers-by in the process.[4]

Although the government's tools for repression were firmly in place, growing discontent with arrests, detentions, political killings and 'cover-ups' led to the creation of a small but active underground opposition inside Malawi.

Three weeks before the bishops' letter was read out, a highly critical letter condemning the activities of Mr Tembo was faxed to all embassies, permanent secretaries, the Army Commander and the Inspector General of Police. The letter was written in response to a BBC World Service interview with Mr Tembo.

During the interview Mr Tembo defended Malawi's one-party political system and referred to exiled critics as "confusionists who are jealous of the peace and calm, law and order reigning in Malawi".[5]

Entitled *An Open letter to Hon John Tembo*, it accused the

minister of telling lies: "Are you really telling the truth that people in this country are free to express their views on any subject? How can you make such statements? No Malawian in this country is free to express his or her view or opinion. Merely to express a view is to go to prison. Yet you choose to lie shamefully to the world."

Aware of Mr Tembo's part in the disappearance of capable politicians who threatened his ambition to become President, the authors of the letter accused him of political murder: "People have been killed because of you. You personally ordered the killings of Gadama, Matenje, Sangala and Chiwanga. Do you think people have forgotten this? Your time is gone. There is no place for you in Malawi's future."

Voicing frustration with nearly 30 years of autocratic rule, the letter ended with a rallying call for greater democracy: "You must let the ordinary people speak. We want multi-party democracy and we are determined to get it. We are going to oppose you to the bitter end."

It seems the letter originated within Malawi. Brown Mpinganjira, Chief Information Officer (1985–86), spent four and a half years in Mikuyu prison. "I was never told the reason for my arrest and when I was released in February 1991, I joined a small group of dissatisfied Malawians. Unwilling to mention names, Mr Mpinganjira admitted the letter to Tembo was written in Zomba and someone smuggled the letter to Zambia, and from there it was faxed back into Malawi."[6]

The letter – the first of its kind to circulate within Malawi – prepared the ground for another letter by the same group. The second letter, entitled *Martyrs' Day*, was faxed from Lusaka to Malawi on 3 March 1992.[7]

The main thrust of the letter is summed up in one of the paragraphs: "The very word 'martyr' needs to be thought about. If a martyr is someone who is imprisoned and tortured or dies for a sincerely held belief, does that mean that the only Malawian martyrs are the ones who suffered before independence? Are there not many innocent Malawians who could be called 'The New Martyrs', especially the ones who have suffered after 1964?"

Circulation was limited to embassies and government officials. The letters were not signed and the government suspected disgruntled exiles.

Five days later the bishops' letter appeared and publicly re-echoed the criticisms found in these two letters.

However, it presented a more detailed critical analysis of the state of the country. The crucial fact was that it was signed by Malawians within Malawi.

Chapter 3

The Bishops' Letter

3.1 Background Information

The Catholic church had remained silent throughout Banda's brutal repressive rule since independence in 1964. So, what prompted the Catholic bishops to speak out in March 1992?

Mgr John Roche, chairman of the committee that drafted the letter, outlined several reasons for writing the letter.[1]

KUKHALA MOYO MCHIKHULUPIRIRO CHATHU

Kalata
ya
maEpisikopi aChikatolika m'Malawi

Lenti 1992

"The election in Zambia (May 1991) surprised a lot of people in Malawi, especially that President Kaunda listened to the voice of the people.

"The changing world order where we see a move towards greater democratisation. This affected Malawi because increasingly Malawians would listen to broadcasting services like the BBC World Service and they were aware of these happenings.

"Among the Christian communities in Malawi there was a growing realisation that issues of human rights and of justice were integral to the gospel message. As

Christians we must be seen to be proclaiming justice and working for human rights.

"As bishops we had been looking at a number of issues such as health-care, education and human rights over the last two years. The letter is the result of all these deliberations which were going on within the bishops' Conference.

"When the Pope met the bishops privately as a group in Malawi (May 1989), he encouraged us to identify areas of injustice."[2]

On 24 January 1992, the Episcopal Conference of Malawi (ECM) met in Lilongwe. All the bishops – five Malawians and one European – listened to a verbal report by three bishops who had met Mr Michael Mlambala, Minister of Education and Culture, to discuss improving partnership in education between the Church and State.[3]

The report revealed a sense of continued frustration with the government. "On monetary matters they (the government) were keen to involve the churches," said Mgr Roche. "When it came to quality of education they felt the church should have no say." Two previous meetings had proved ineffective and Mgr Roche summed up the situation: "Partnership meant pay up and shut up."

Planning the letter – 1992

21 January	Bishops meet in Lilongwe and decide to write a critical letter about the state of the country
28 January	Drafting committee starts work on the first copy
11 February	Drafting committee meets again
18 February	Bishops approve and sign the letter
21 February	The letter is printed at Montfort Press in Balaka
3 March	The bishops call their priests to explain the letter
8 March	The letter is read in Catholic churches throughout Malawi

Mgr Roche pointed to under-financed health-care facilities as another example: "Missionary medical hospitals provided at least 50% of medical care for the whole country but were given only 6% of the budget."

The bishops decided to act by writing a letter exposing unjust government policy in several areas of Malawian life. Mgr John Roche was appointed chairman of the drafting committee together with three Malawians and three expatriates.[4]

Although wrongly accused by the government of being "the brains" behind the letter, Mgr Roche's enthusiasm helped to bring the whole operation together. "I was totally convinced that the time was right. In the past there had been pastoral letters on baptism, repentance, conversion, but this was the first one on social issues," he said. "Our silence in the past was a scandal."

On 28 January, Mgr Roche met the drafting committee and explained the areas the bishops wanted to address. "The central question we tackled was, what does our faith call us to today in Malawi," said Mgr Roche. "That's why we called it *Living Our Faith*. The heart of the document is the expression, 'The dignity of every human person is sacred'."

The six committee members agreed to write on a particular area and they met again on 11 February. Two days later the letter was ready and Mgr Roche presented it at an emergency meeting of the ECM on 18 February.

Archbishop James Chiona, chairman of the ECM, described the letter as "an excellent document". The bishops recommended the inclusion of more local Chichewa proverbs and agreed that the letter be read out in all Catholic parishes and outstations on the first Sunday of Lent (8 March). By midday the letter was ready for printing.[5]

The next difficulty; how to avoid the letter being leaked. The Catholic church owned two print works, Likuni in Lilongwe and Montfort Press in Blantyre. Since government informers had infiltrated most workplaces, Mgr Roche suggested the use of a smaller publishing house in Balaka.[6]

It belonged to the Montfort Missionaries and Fr Pierre Gamba, the workshop manager, willingly accepted to print the letter. No Malawians were directly involved to avoid the risk of someone informing MCP officials.

A total of 16,000 copies were printed; 10,000 in Chichewa; 5,000 in Tumbuka and 1,000 in English. Chichewa is the most widely spoken language in Malawi. Tumbuka is spoken mainly in the north while about 10% of the people speak English.[7]

3.2 Content of the Letter

Living Our Faith, an 11-page pastoral letter, began with a quote from Pope Paul VI's encyclical, *The Evangelisation of Peoples*: "The church is certainly not willing to restrict her action to the religious field and disassociate herself from man's temporal problems."[8]

Having established their right to speak on matters of human life and activity, the bishops listed several areas of concern.

- *Increasing inequality between the rich and poor*: "One reason for this is the deplorable wage structure which exists. For many the wages they receive are grossly inadequate ... We wish to state that every person has a right to a just reward for work done... At the same time a minority enjoys the fruits of development and can afford to live in luxury and wealth. We appeal for a more just and equal distribution of the nation's wealth."

- *The spread of corruption*: "Bribery and nepotism are growing in political, economic and social life. This causes violence and harm to the spirit."

- *Serious flaws within the education system*: "There remains a large-scale problem of illiteracy in our society. It must be recognised that this is a problem that cannot be solved by state initiatives alone ... It must be recognised that standards of education are actually falling. Schools are grossly overcrowded and suffer from a serious lack of teachers... Access to education should not depend on whom the candidate knows nor how much money he possesses."

- *Cutbacks in Health-care* : "Without doubt the most serious problem is the acute shortage of health centres to cater for the population. This will demand allocation of more resources from the state." The quality of medical care was described as "seriously inadequate".

- *Basic freedoms denied*: "Academic freedom is seriously restricted; exposing injustices can be considered a betrayal; revealing some evils of our society is seen as slandering the country; monopoly of mass media and censorship prevent the expression of dissenting views; some people have paid dearly for their political opinions; access to public places like markets, hospitals, bus depots... is frequently denied to those who cannot produce a party card; forced donations have become a way of life."

- *Blatant injustices*; "We cannot ignore or turn a blind eye to our peoples' experience of unfairness and injustice. For example, those who, losing their land without fair compensation, are deprived of their livelihood, or those who are imprisoned without knowing when their cases will be heard."

- *Inadequacies in the judicial system*: "We call upon all and particularly those responsible for the administration of justice to ensure not only that procedures are respected but also that impartial judgement is rendered to the accused person."

The letter proposed the removal of government influence over the judiciary since fairness "will only be possible if the (judicial) administration is independent of external influence, political or otherwise".

To balance their statements the bishops began each section with tributes to what had been achieved. For example: "We applaud the efforts which have been made by the government to provide education at all levels." and "particularly worthy of mention has been the establishment of an excellent system of primary health care."

Partnership was emphasised: "Only through a mutual recognition of rights and responsibilities will a fruitful partnership between the Church and State be realised in practice."

The bishops were confident of public support: "People will not be scandalised to hear these things, they know them. Feeding them slogans and half truths – or untruths – only increases their cynicism and their mistrust of government."

The letter ended with an impassioned appeal to fellow Christians "to respond to this state of affairs and work towards a change of climate. Participation in the life of the country is not only a right, it is also a duty that each Christian should be proud to assume and exercise responsibly."

(Extracts from *Living Our Faith*)

Mgr Roche insists the letter was not intended to be a political statement but "a genuine pastoral response to the sad state of affairs in the country". He explained that the term 'a change of climate' referred to the need for "a serious ongoing dialogue to resolve problems together".

Mgr Joseph Zuza, Secretary General of the ECM, distributed the letter to the bishops. On 3 March all Catholic parish priests were called to the residence of their respective bishops and told to read the letter on 8 March.

Ironically, the next day all the bishops met Banda at Sanjika palace in Blantyre. The bishops had arranged the meeting in early January in order to present Mgr Tarcisius Ziyaye, the newly elected bishop for Dedza. Their courtesy visit proved an embarrassing mistake.

The Catholic church at Magomero nearly exposed the secret

operation by reading the letter during the Ash Wednesday celebration on 4 March – four days before the agreed date.

Stephen Chapman, a lay missionary volunteer, was in Sitima church in southern Malawi when the letter was read: "Because the letter was so long, three different people read it and I got the impression that people didn't want to miss a word of it. When a pertinent statement was made you could hear a lot of shuffling and coughing."

Fr Gamba celebrated mass in a rural parish near Balaka and noted how young people clapped at various parts of the letter but "older members remained quiet". Nearly 30 years of vigorous repression meant that interest and enthusiasm for the letter was tinged with a tangible fear of possible government revenge.

3.3 Immediate Government Reaction

Predictably, Banda reacted angrily to the letter and to the fact that he had met the bishops only a few days earlier.

During an interview on MBC (9 March) he questioned the bishops' integrity: "I was shocked to see that the very same bishops who had praised me to the sky, saying they were praying for me, said the opposite two to three days later. That is double-crossing. Is that Christianity? Would Jesus Christ do a thing like that?"[9]

Mgr Roche admits the meeting with Banda on 4 March was a mistake. But he explained that it was impossible for the bishops to air their grievances with Banda on that day because the meeting – as with most audiences with Banda – was being broadcast live on MBC.

Events moved swiftly. On 10 March the bishops were interrogated for eight hours at Kanjedza police station in Blantyre. When they left, they were ordered to remain at the Archbishop's house until further notice.[10]

The Inspector General of Police issued a press release on 11 March declaring the bishops' letter to be a seditious document:

"Anyone who bought, received, procured or otherwise got hold of the said episcopal letter, should surrender it to the nearest police station. Continued circulation of the letter or possession of it, is in itself sedition and will result in criminal prosecution."

Section 50 of the Penal Code – the offence of sedition – is defined as an intention "to bring hatred or contempt or excite disaffection against the person of the President, or the government". Such a law – unacceptable in most countries – is described by Martin Hill of Amnesty International as part of Malawi's "legal framework of repression". The government used the law extensively during the first weeks to arrest hundreds of Malawians who kept the letter.[11]

Frequent radio announcements repeated the content of the press release. Chairmen and secretaries of parish councils were asked to attend a meeting with the MCP regional chairman in Lilongwe on 12 March. Many priests were chairmen of their parish councils and attended the meeting.

Fr Joseph de Gabriel travelled from Zomba to the Lilongwe meeting: "The MCP chairman shouted at the people and tried to intimidate them. When the bishops' secretary stood up to complain they took him outside. Our parishioners said nothing and none of them stayed for the free lunch."

The government's initial tactic was to set the people against the bishops. Parts of the MCP National Executive report were read out on the lunchtime news (12 March): "The bishops are hypocrites, deceitful, full of double standards. They are destroying the peace and tranquillity of our country. The Christians are shocked and dismayed with their lying ways. Their aim seems to be the foundation of another Christian Liberation Party. Malawians do not accept the views of the bishops."[12]

The next bulletin began with the statement: "The President is happy because the Christians are behind him and not behind the bishops."

The editorial page of *Malawi News* (14 March) carried a scath-

	Diary of Events: 8–19 March 1992
8 March	The bishops' letter was read out in Catholic churches throughout Malawi.
10 March	Catholic bishops taken to Kanjedza police station in Blantyre. Interrogated for eight hours by the Police Commissioner. Told to remain at the Archbishop's house.
11 March	The letter declared a seditious document. It was a criminal offence to keep a copy.
	At an emergency executive MCP meeting in Lilongwe senior party officials plotted to kill the bishops.
12 March	Meeting of parish council chairpersons and secretaries.
14 March	An editorial in *Malawi News* entitled 'No Mercy' condemned the bishops and Mgr Roche in particular.
15 March	Catholic churches packed. In Zomba university students marched to the cathedral. After the mass they gathered at the town centre singing hymns in support of the bishops. Several students arrested then released.
16 March	Zomba university students marched through the town centre. The police used tear gas to disperse them.
17 March	Parliament opened. Banda made no mention of the bishops' letter.
	Polytechnic students rioted in Blantyre. More than 60 students arrested.
19 March	About 20 members of the MYP burnt down part of Montfort Press in Balaka where the letter was printed.

ing attack against the bishops. Entitled 'Cloaks of Deceit', it branded the bishops as cowards: "It is deceit of the highest order to go to somebody's house, praise him to the highest heavens for the good he does to you, and then turn round and speak ill of the same person."[13]

Mgr Roche, identified as the mastermind behind the letter, was accused of introducing IRA tactics into Malawi. "Roche himself is Irish. And who does not know the problems Irishmen have at home? Instead of being grateful for being given an opportunity to come here and work, he is bent on practising IRA atrocities on innocent church-goers."[14]

The front page headline, 'Party Condemns Catholic Bishops', reported the conclusions of the emergency MCP meeting: "Delegates therefore resolved to condemn unreservedly the attempt by the bishops to enter politics and use the pulpit to sow seeds of confusion in Malawi and to disturb the peace, stability, progress and hard won freedom which has been achieved under the wise and dynamic leadership of the Ngawzi."[15]

Government over-reaction to the letter stemmed from newspaper guidelines to suppress any criticism of Banda.[16]

Two days of student protests at Zomba University (15–16 March) resulted in its closure. Student riots spread to Blantyre where the polytechnic was closed on 18 March and 62 students arrested.[17]

The paramilitary wing of the MYP set fire to the Montfort Press in Balaka where the letter was printed. Fr Gamba watched the attack from a nearby building: "The young pioneers started smashing the place. Word soon spread and students with parishioners came while the press was in flames. They beat up some pioneers who tried to escape." The next day the police arrived and reported the incident as a burglary.[18]

Apart from 16,000 printed copies, it is difficult to estimate exactly how many copies of the letter were in circulation. Over-worked photocopy machines were used to cope with popular demand.

3.4 Plot to Kill the Bishops

An emergency meeting of MCP senior officials met in Lilongwe on 11 March to discuss the letter. MBC recorded the meeting and tape recordings of the meeting were smuggled to London. They revealed plans by some officials to kill the bishops.

Wadson Deleza, Administrative Secretary of the MCP, chaired the meeting with Mr Tembo and declared: "According to our tradition, once we have killed someone we don't go back to the President to announce we have done so. We just keep quiet."

Katola Phiri, Minister of Local Government, made an explicit demand: "These bishops should be killed. Whoever has gone against Kamuzu should be killed." He added: "If I could meet one of the bishops anytime, whether day or night, he would disappear. Our hearts will not rest until we hear that all the seven bishops do not exist any more."

Charles Kamphulusa, chairman of the MCP Blanytre branch, was determined to see the bishops killed: "If we were given guns we could have killed them ourselves. These bishops are great sinners. They are drunkards, womanisers, thieves."

Some women delegates were equally forceful in condemning the bishops. Margaret Chiponda, a member of the Lilongwe Women's League, said: "These bishops should not be allowed to preach any more. Actually, to make things easier we just have to kill these bishops."

Hilda Manjamkhosi, chairwoman of the MCP Lilongwe branch, described the bishops as "stupid" and declared: "We do not want this Catholic church any more, and these bishops should be killed right away."

"I want these bishops killed tonight," said Cecilia Kankodo, chairwoman of Dedza MCP branch. "These bishops should go to the unknown because we do not want them. They are bad people."

Mr Deleza concluded the meeting: "I would say that these seven

INTERNATIONAL SECRETARIAT
1 Easton Street London WC1X 8DJ
United Kingdom

EXTERNAL (for general distribution)

AI Index: AFR 36/06/92
Distr: UA/SC

Please bring this action to the attention of the person in your section responsible for outreach work as it is felt that appeals from church organizations may be particularly effective.

UA 90/92   Fear of Extrajudicial Execution   16 March 1992
MALAWI   Archbishop James CHIONA, Roman Catholic Archbishop of
                    Blantyre
            Bishop F MKHORI   }
            Bishop M A CHIMOLE   }
            Bishop A ASSOLARI   } Roman Catholic bishops
            Bishop A CHAMGWERA   }
            Bishop G M CHISENDERA   }
            Monsignor John ROCHE   }

people are finished. They will be killed. They should not be found anywhere in this country because they will be killed. A ghost can go to them and warn them about our agreement but still they will be killed. Today these seven people are going. They will be killed."[19]

The MCP meeting finished at 4 p.m. Mr Tembo left immediately in order to inform Banda about the recommendation of the MCP officials to have the bishops killed.

However, someone at the meeting informed the German embassy about the decision to kill the bishops. The German ambassador alerted the other embassies. Mgr Roche was in Lilongwe that afternoon. He received a telephone call asking him to go immediately to the British High Commission. When he arrived he was told about the threat to his life and stayed there a few days.

Two days later, one of the MCP officials who attended the meeting, managed to smuggle a letter to London. The letter contained details of the decision to kill the bishops. Within hours the BBC World Service programme *Focus on Africa*, reported the proposed plot. The story was repeated throughout that day on several BBC news bulletins.

BBC World Service programmes are popular in Malawi. Coverage of the plot to kill the bishops exposed the intention of senior MCP officials. Such exposure combined with mounting pressure from the British, German and American governments prevented the MCP from acting too hastily.

The government had killed critics in the past, even whole families. But did they seriously intend to kill seven bishops?

"I don't think there was an elaborate plan to kill the bishops," argues BBC correspondent Mike Hall. "The ruling MCP is a fanatical party and party officials owe their positions, their jobs, their income, their livelihood to Banda. I think the decision that the bishops should be killed was really an expression of collective fanaticism which one finds in the MCP party."

Similar doubts were expressed by Richard Carver of Amnesty International. "It was difficult to know the precise threat to the bishops. We knew that the government had killed three cabinet ministers in 1983, and in 1989 they killed a Malawian journalist, his two wives and seven children in a fire-bomb attack in Lusaka. It had happened before and so we took the threat very seriously."

Mr Carver was not surprised by government reaction to the bishops' letter. "There had been no public expression of dissent since independence until the letter. That's why the government reaction was such a frenzied one, because this was the first time they had to confront public criticism."

By labelling the letter 'seditious' and issuing death threats against the bishops, the government helped fuel its impact. Internal and international support for the letter gained momentum.

3.5 Internal Reaction to the Letter

The bishops received widespread support within Malawi, especially from non-Catholics.

Muhammad Kulesi, Secretary General of the Muslim Association in Malawi, said: "It was an honest letter that came at the right time. It talked about what was happening in Malawi and needed no imagination." He sent a private letter of support to Archbishop Chiona because "they [the Muslims] could not come out", said Mr Kulesi.

Rev Aaron Longwe, a Church of Scotland minister, remarked that the letter "represented the feelings of the people of Malawi. It spoke on our behalf and has become the voice to the voiceless."

Margaret Banda, an Anglican and no relation to Banda, felt uplifted by the letter: "The letter was excellent and the people who wrote it should be blessed by God. Everyone is tired of this government."

Aleke Banda, former MCP Secretary General – also unrelated to Banda – referred to the letter as a "terrific and thorough job. Malawi has never been the same." Mr Mordechai Msisha, chairman of the Malawi Law Society echoed similar sentiments: "The bishops opened our throats."

Jack Mapanje, the country's leading poet and now resident in Britain, said: "Malawians needed opposition from within the country and the bishops' letter must be seen as a turning point in the build-up of opposition that preceded it. The fact that it was read in homes in the north and south on the same day showed how it spread like fire."

Ardent government supporters like Tony Mita, Chief Information Office, declined to comment. When asked to reply to the content of the letter, he replied: "The bishops are safe."

3.6 Malawian Catholic Support

Initial attempts by the press to discredit the bishops as "confusionists" failed to lessen Catholic support for the bishops. Malawian Catholics expressed their solidarity by packing Catholic churches for weeks after the letter.

Fr Henry Masuka kept a detailed diary of events. His entry for

15 March read: "Zomba cathedral was packed with Catholic and non-Catholics. The collection was double. Zomba university students marched on the town centre singing hymns in support of the bishops. After mass they marched back through Zomba joined by the nurses at the hospital; 7–8 were arrested for 20 minutes. Shots were fired into the air to disperse them. Disturbances lasted into the evening with students chanting for a multi-party system."

Fr Gamba faxed a similar message to London the same day: "While returning from mass, the university students started singing – Ndakulakwirani chiyani, fuko langa lokondeka (What have they done to my people?). They sang other songs like 'Tikufuna multi-party' (We want multi-party). Five anti-riot cars arrived at the campus but students stood in front of the guns and started throwing stones."

Malawi's Catholic Students' Organization (CSO) wrote a leaflet in support of the letter: "Undoubtedly the pastoral letter will go down in our history as the most soul-searching document on current realities in Malawi that has ever come out. It is a light for the years ahead."

Local and expatriate priests from all seven dioceses expressed their support. The Lilongwe Diocesan Council of Priests (DCOP) conveyed a common message: "We express gratitude for your pastoral letter. You know that we support whole-heartedly your teaching which is the teaching of the church. We pledge our unreserved commitment to keep on sharing it with our Christians."[20]

"The letter is not against or at war with anybody but wants to state clearly that it is time to recognise publicly all that is being said privately in meetings, talks and discussions," said Fr Gamba. "It is not presenting something new."

Archbishop Chiona said he feared for his life after the letter was published. He was surprised by what he terms the government's "exaggerated response" and added: "There were positive things in the letter. But we did not anticipate the government would act as it did. The letter put things in gear. It has changed completely the atmosphere. The people have received the letter whole-heartedly. All Malawians appreciate it."

"The bishops have opened our throats" was a commonly heard expression. Paul O' Hagan, a volunteer missionary, still remembers his surprise at the people's vocal reaction: "Before the letter no one talked politics. It was too risky. Not even a husband and wife talked about it. Somehow the letter released them."

3.7 International Support

Government over-reaction to the letter and failure to realise that the Catholic church within Malawi was part of a larger international organisation fuelled even greater publicity for the letter and its content.

Unlike private individuals, the bishops had the support of the wider international Catholic community. Within a week, 17 episcopal conferences throughout the world responded to caustic newspaper editorials and rumoured death threats with faxed messages of support for their fellow bishops.

In Britain, Cardinal Basil Hume, chairman of the Bishops' Conference of England and Wales, spoke of his "grave concern" over developments in Malawi.

Other Christian churches complained to Banda. The Archbishop of Canterbury, Dr George Carey, requested that "the bishops' safety be guaranteed and they are given the full protection of the law".[21]

The Church of Scotland – of which Banda claimed to be an elder – wrote a personal attack on Banda: "The church strongly disassociates itself from statements reportedly made by Dr Banda." The letter ended: "We welcome the bishops' call for more people participation in the life of Malawi."[22]

The US Episcopal Conference sent a letter to James Baker, the then US Secretary of State: "The detention of Catholic bishops in response to a pastoral letter defending basic human rights is an abominable act and it is the latest in a long series of violations of decency by a dictator whose people have suffered abuse and deprivation for years."[23]

The US government did not issue any public response to the protests but waited until the Paris meeting of Western donors in May.[24]

Lynda Chalker, Minister for Overseas Development, in reply to a letter sent by Nicholas Scott, Conservative MP for Jersey, said: "We have told the Malawian authorities that lack of government accountability and respect for human rights in Malawi will increasingly influence the overall size and composition of our bilateral aid programme. We have already reduced substantially the amount of balance of payments we have pledged to Malawi from £10m to £5m."[25]

The European Parliament discussed the situation of human rights in Malawi and issued a statement: "We welcome the courageous attitude of the Malawi Catholic bishops and all those – whether belonging to the church or not – who made their criticism of current trends in Malawi politics public."[26]

In a letter to Banda, Ken Coates, a member of the European Parliament (MEP), reminded him that the European Parliament "has closely monitored human rights abuses in Malawi" and called for "the safety of the signatories of the pastoral letter".[27]

Henry Chiwaya, chairperson of MAC, was not surprised by the overwhelming positive response to the letter: "It came from within the country and it started something irreversible."

3.8 The Media

Four days before the bishops' letter was read out, I received a faxed copy of the bishops' letter from Malawi with instructions to "get it on the BBC". The reason was simple: "We need their protection."

Having spent ten years in Malawi, I realised the danger for those involved if the letter was discovered. I arranged a secret meeting with a BBC reporter and he agreed to remain silent until the letter was read out.

On March 9, BBC *Network Africa* carried a five-minute report about the letter while the BBC World Service mentioned it in hourly news bulletins. With a potential listening audience of 120 million people, the Malawi government was unable to act in secret.

"If the BBC had not responded as soon as they did, I feel we could have been in worse trouble," said Mgr Roche. "Somehow we felt safe that the outside world knew what we had done."

It is now acknowledged that media coverage on the BBC World Service and in the British press played a vital role in preventing the government from acting too harshly with the bishops.

Interest in Malawi escalated. BBC *Network Africa* is a weekday news programme broadcasting to English-speaking Africa four times a day. Only three items on Malawi were broadcast in a three-month period before 8 March, compared with 26 stories during the same period after the letter.[28]

Robin White, editor of BBC *Focus on Africa*, a daily news and current affairs programme, remarked how increased interest in Malawi led some BBC reporters to joke about renaming the programme 'Focus on Malawi'. A survey of British newspapers reveals that in a six-month period before the letter only three articles were written about Malawi. But, in the following two-month period, a total of 31 articles appeared in the British broadsheets.[29]

Mr Hall filed regular reports for the BBC about events surrounding the bishops' letter. "The publicity from the letter fuelled a lot of media interest. Before the letter, Malawi was not really covered." He had no doubts about its impact: "People will see 8 March as the beginning of a whole process of change."[30] Melinda Ham wrote reports for Associated Press (AP) in Lusaka and saw the letter as "a very courageous move" and "a watershed in Malawian politics".

Fax machines were invaluable in sidestepping the long-established government practice of tapping telephone calls and opening letters.

The government could not disconnect all business fax machines without damaging the economic activity of the country. They proved to be a quick and safe means of circulating information outside Malawi and within the country. As Mr Hall remarked: "No sooner had the ink of the pastoral letter dried than it was being read all over the world."

Chapter 4

Formation of Opposition Groups

The bishops were keen for other groups to take the lead and remove some of the pressure on them. They were tired and frightened from having to sleep in different parish centres to avoid possible MYP reprisals.[1]

Brown Mpinganjira, former Information Officer (1985–86), argues that the letter sent a clear signal to exiled opposition groups: "The fact that the bishops survived gave courage and strength to government opponents inside and outside the country."

Chakufwa Chihana, Secretary General of the Southern Africa Trade Union Co-ordination Council (SATUCC) – imprisoned for advocating multi-party democracy in Malawi during the seventies – was the first opposition figure to openly support the bishops' letter.[2]

"The Catholic bishops have started the ball rolling. Their pastoral letter calmly and accurately reflected the deep social, economic and political problems our country faces," Mr Chihana commented during a BBC interview on 13 March 1992.[3]

Chihana was in defiant mood when he gave the keynote speech during a pro-democracy meeting of exiled Malawians in Lusaka on 22 March 1992. Entitled *'Prospects for Democracy in Malawi'*, he criticised the autocratic style of Banda's regime: "The immediate history of our country shows the gross abuse of basic human rights, growing poverty and mass starvation, personalised rule and total tyranny by the leadership that brought independence to Malawi."

Describing Banda's manipulation of the MCP as "twentieth century feudalism", he complained that after 28 years of independence "Malawi still remains the poorest country in the region where mass poverty, starvation, nepotism, tribalism and fanatical mob-politics remain the order of the day."

He called on Malawians "to stand up to one of the worst dictatorships in Africa. All of us must unite and change things for the better. If we can do that, then we will be sending a clear message to Dr Banda that the time has come for him to step aside so that a new and vibrant democratic Malawi can be built."

The Interim Committee for a Democratic Alliance (ICDA) was formed during the Lusaka meeting (20–22 March 1992) with the aim of campaigning for human rights and democracy in Malawi. Chihana was elected chairman.

A press release described ICDA as having no particular ideology: "Its purpose is to help bring about a political atmosphere in which all Malawians can discuss politics openly without fear of recrimination. The immediate objective is to fight for the restoration of human rights in Malawi, the release of all political prisoners and a general amnesty for all exiles."

ICDA began printing a fortnightly newsletter, *The Malawi Democrat*, in order to increase publicity and support for ICDA. Although printed in Lusaka, it was mainly distributed around Malawi.[4]

Conference delegates asked Chihana to return to Malawi and organise a national conference of political forces within the country. Chihana arrived at Kamuzu International airport in Lilongwe on 6 April 1992. The police arrested him on the airport tarmac as he read a prepared statement in support of multi-party democracy.

Malawi News devoted its front page to Chihana's arrest. The headline, 'Chihana: A nobody to Malawians', conveyed the government's intention to discredit his growing popularity.

"What surprises many Malawians is that they have never heard of this man until the BBC started making news out of his seditious activities. Chihana is an unknown entity in this country. He has no following and therefore his claim that he represents Malawians who are against Kamuzu, the party and the government, has no substance." (*Malawi News*, 11–17 April 1992). Chihana spent most of the next 14 months in prison, first at Zomba and then at Mikuyu prison, from 16 July 1992 to 10 June 1993.

Chihana told a delegation of British lawyers who visited him at Mikuyu in September 1992 about his prison treatment: "The cell is very small. It is only about the size of my body. There is a window in the cell which has been deliberately blocked off. There is no ventilation. Their intention is that I should suffocate. I was held for almost one month in leg irons. My legs swelled. I cannot see my family and friends."

Alliance for Democracy (AFORD) declared itself an opposition group on 1 May 1992, with Chihana as chairman and Henry Chiume as vice-chairman.[6] The government began arresting AFORD supporters. Rev Aaron Longwe, then AFORD's Vice-Publicity Secretary, was arrested on several occasions for promoting multi-party democracy.

During his first arrest Rev Longwe was taken to the punishment cell at Maula Prison. "They locked me inside a small cell. There was another prisoner tied to a peg in the centre of the room. Any slight movement and he screamed with pain." On another occasion he ate nothing during three days of imprisonment because the prison wardens "were experts in poisoning techniques".

Amnesty International adopted Chihana and Rev Longwe as prisoners of conscience and campaigned for their release. Several separate BBC interviews with both men helped to increase international recognition of their situation.

Another opposition group, the United Democratic Front (UDF), was launched at a meeting in Lilongwe on 21 March 1992.[7]

Mr Mpinganjira, UDF Publicity Secretary, describes how UDF started as an underground movement: "A group of 12 dissatisfied Malawians first met at a house in Zomba in October 1991. Ways of opposing the dictatorship were discussed but we were afraid of

MALAWI ON TRIAL!
LILONGWE HIGH COURT, MAY 6TH 1992

FREE CHAKUFWA CHIHANA

"For the past thirty years we have been denied freedoms which so many other nations have taken for granted.... We have been denied our right to elect a government and leaders of our choice. We have been intimidated and victimised. We must now say 'enough is enough'. We demand to join other free nations of this world." *Chakufwa Chihana, 6 April 1992*

DO YOU WANT TO BE FREE? HOW LONG WILL YOU KEEP QUIET? CALL FOR CHIHANA'S FREEDOM AT LILONGWE HIGH COURT, MAY 6TH

"It will, of course, be claimed by the Malawi Congress Party that this call amounts to an act of sedition. I tell you it is not. It is a genuine call for freedom..... There comes a time in the history of every nation when all must recognise that change is not only desirable, but inevitable. For Malawi, THAT TIME IS NOW! Let all Malawians have a say in their future, freely and without hinderance and fear. Let us hold a referendum.

"The destiny of our country cannot and should never be left in the hands of a sole political party or one individual. There should be no recrimination, no witchhunt, against any group or tribe. *We must unite in a democratic alliance*... The choice before us is simple: are we going to remain in slavery under a dictatorship or choose to join the ranks of free nations?"

"We must stand up and be counted. The struggle for democracy begins now!"

FROM THE INTERIM COMMITTEE FOR A DEMOCRATIC ALLIANCE
Campaigning for human rights and democracy in Malawi

Government Attempts to Silence Chihana

1 March 1992	Chihana questioned by police for six hours before leaving Malawi for Zambia.
19–20 March	Chihana addressed a pro-democracy conference in Lusaka, Zambia. He called for a non-violent campaign to bring multi-party democracy to Malawi.
6 April	Chihana returned to Malawi. Arrested on the tarmac of Kamuzu International airport while reading a prepared script. Detained at Zomba Prison.
11 July	Released on bail.
13 July	Charged on three accounts of possessing and importing seditious material including the bishops' letter.
14 July	Re-arrested in Lilongwe. Taken to Mikuyu Prison.
13 September	Visited by a delegation of British lawyers.
14 December	Found guilty of sedition. Sentenced to two years imprisonment. Refused bail pending his appeal.
29 March 1993	Chihana's appeal dismissed by Chief Justice Richard Banda. Sentence reduced to 9 months' imprisonment.
12 June	Chihana released from prison.[5]

infiltration and so agreed that membership would be by invitation only."

Membership increased after the bishops' letter. Aleke Banda argues that UDF received greater support than AFORD because it did not restrict its membership: "By excluding former MCP members, AFORD created an exclusive enclave along tribal lines. We all had MCP party cards and so everyone in the past was virtually a paid-up member of MCP."

On 19 October, UDF was declared an official opposition party. Bakili Muluzi, a businessman and former Secretary General of the MCP was elected chairman. AFORD had been declared an opposition party a month earlier with Chihana as chairman.

Initially, the majority of AFORD supporters were northerners, while UDF supporters included Malawians from all regions. Many former MCP ministers joined UDF.[8]

AFORD and UDF had one common aim: the suspension of the Constitution's Article 4 which enshrined the status of the MCP as the sole legal party. Its withdrawal was essential for the creation of multi-party democracy within Malawi.[9]

Mr Mpinganjira admits to a lack of unity between the opposition groups: "It's a situation where the right hand does not know what the left is doing. By not being united it gives the MCP more chance to be voted back into office."

But the emergence of UDF and AFORD continued the bishops' call for a 'change of climate.' "The Church cannot spearhead the campaign to restore democracy to Malawi. That must be left to the likes of Mr Chihana," said the Right Rev Mathias Chimole, Bishop of Lilongwe.

"Opposition groups would have surfaced without the bishops' letter," argues Aleke Banda. "It would have been bloodier but inevitable." He admits that "the letter was a source of great strength to the pressure groups and probably brought forward their existence by at least 10 years."

Bishop Chimole explained why the Catholic church failed to speak out in favour of Chihana: "We cannot say one political system is better, or support the actions of an individual."

Chapter 5

Factory Strikes

Popular reaction to the bishops' letter and the subsequent emergence of the two opposition groups, AFORD and UDF, began to erode the climate of fear that had stifled criticism of Banda's 28 years of totalitarian rule. Both events prepared the way for a three-day strike by Blantyre factory workers.

The bishops' letter had urged the government to increase wages: "Though many basic goods and materials are available, they are beyond the means of our people. One of the reasons for this is the deplorable wage structure which exists."

But the government – having labelled the letter as seditious – made no attempt to address the issue of wage increases. Growing frustration among Malawian workers erupted on the morning of 5 May 1992.

The overnight shift at David Whitehead's textile factory in Blantyre switched off their machines and began picketing for better wages outside the factory gates. Four hours later the police arrived and dispersed the protestors.[1]

Malawi's first strike since independence in 1964 continued the next day when hundreds of Whitehead workers marched through the city centre shouting slogans demanding better wages.

As they passed other factories and offices, hundreds of Malawians poured out of their workplaces and joined the demonstration.

Frank Mayinga, co-editor of *The Malawi Democrat*, described what happened next: "The march ended up outside the police headquarters on Kamuzu Highway. The police tried to disperse them with teargas. The crowds fought running battles with the police who turned from teargas to firing in the air to disperse the crowds. The firing continued well after dark."[2]

Margaret Twist, whose husband was one of the expatriate managers at Whitehead's, spent the day locked in her Blantyre home: "We heard machine-gun fire. Then crowds of people came up our street, overturned a car and tried to fight off the police. After a short while, tanks were stationed at both ends of our road. The paramilitary were everywhere. It was very frightening."

Clashes with the police continued the next day and the police mobile force surrounded Banda's Sanjika palace. "Much of the damage and the deaths occurred when it became clear the police were tired and losing their patience," said Mr Mayinga. Thirty-eight people died and hundreds were injured during the two-day riot.[3]

Strikes spread to Lilongwe (185 miles north of Blanytre) where hundreds of tobacco workers threw bottles and stones at Malawi's riot police and blocked roads leading to Kanengo industrial suburb.

In a nationwide radio broadcast Banda called for calm: "I want to appeal to all of you to stay calm and be peaceful. All genuine grievances should be looked into expeditiously and corrective measures taken with speed. Let us all behave like ladies and gentlemen and refrain from damaging property."

"People seemed to respect what they heard," said Mr Mpinganjira. "It was the first caring dialogue since the riots began."

However, the strikes continued. On 12 May, workers on the tea and tobacco plantations in Thyolo and Mulanje in southern Malawi decided to strike, together with sugar plantation workers in Dwanga in the north.

Air Malawi and Malawi Railway workers joined bank workers at the National Bank and the Reserve Bank of Malawi in Lilongwe's city centre to protest for higher wages.

The government tried to stem the rising tide of unrest. On 13 May minimum wage increases for manual workers were announced on the front page of *The Daily Times*: "Wages have been raised from K2.17 to K2.60 per day in the cities of Mzuzu, Blantyre and Lilongwe; in the Municipality of Zomba and all other townships from K1.95 to K2.34, and in all other areas from K1.74 to K2.09." In May 1992, one pound sterling was worth K5.80 Malawi kwacha. Therefore, the increase in minimum wage meant workers still received under 50 pence a day.

Two days later, civil servants received a 40% wage increase with some sectors receiving up to 50%.[4]

The unprecedented wave of strikes throughout Malawi in May 1992 confirmed that the 'culture of fear' – where no-one dared to criticise Banda or the government – was being replaced by an atmosphere of open confrontation with the government.

An editorial in *Malawi News* (16–22 May), pointed the finger at outside interference: "We have evidence that foreign agents were involved in the recent riots in Malawi." The evidence centred on the "large presence of nationals of a particular western country in one of the country's leading hotels who not only acted suspiciously, but were also heard conversing secretly in washrooms about the situation, clearly indicating their involvement".

Banda's popularity reached an all-time low on 15 May when thousands of Malawians boycotted his annual birthday celebration. Instead of the usual full capacity crowd of 25,000, the stadium was sparsely filled with a crowd of around 5,000 people.

"Something irreversible is happening in Malawi," wrote the Right Rev Donald Arden, former Anglican bishop of the Diocese of southern Malawi, after a visit there in mid-May 1992.

Chapter 6

Western Donors Cut Aid

During the cold war, Malawi was favoured by western governments because of its staunch anti-communist foreign policy and espousal of free market doctrines.

However, Douglas Hurd, the Foreign Secretary, indicated a possible change in British policy towards Malawi.

In a speech in June 1990, he declared: "Countries tending towards pluralism, public accountability, respect for human rights and market principles should be encouraged. Governments who persist with repressive policies should not expect us to support their folly."[1]

Four months later, the London-based human rights group, Africa Watch, produced a highly critical 116-page report *Where Silence Rules: The Suppression of Dissent in Malawi* (October 1990). It detailed the systematic suppression of dissent during the 26 years of Banda's rule.

The report concludes: "At a moment when Western governments are loudly proclaiming their universal attachment to human rights and pluralist democracies, they should turn their attention to poor, forgotten Malawi."[2]

Initially, the document failed to persuade the British government to move against the Malawian government. But in July 1991, Lynda Chalker, Minister for Overseas Development, demanded an improvement in Malawi's human rights record and announced a cut in British aid, from £10 million to £5 million.

Amnesty International drew attention to political repression in Malawi by frequent reports on the treatment of political detainees.

Amnesty International compiled a report on the treatment of

prisoners within the country. Entitled *Malawi: Prison conditions, cruel punishment and detention without trial* (February 1992), the report described how prisoners sentenced to the 'hard core programme' are "kept naked and chained to the floor, given minimal food, denied medical care and severely beaten. Many prisoners are reported to have died where this programme is in force."[3]

In April 1992, Amnesty International informed the EC and the Western Donors about the attempt by senior MCP officials to kill the bishops, and the mass arrests that followed the publication of the bishops' letter.[4]

In response to these events, the Western Donors Consultative Group met in Paris on 13 May and decided to freeze all Malawi's 1992/93 aid, because of its poor human rights record and a history of repression under Banda.

But the donors did allocate $170 million in humanitarian aid to help Malawi with the 1992 drought which affected the central and southern regions.[5]

Louis Chimango, Minister of Finance, had asked the donors to consider three points in Malawi's favour; reliably anti-communist policies, pro-South Africa, and old friendship.[6]

The donors were unmoved and refused the Malawian government request for $74 million in non-humanitarian assistance. The suspension was to last six months, with the possibility of an extension if the government failed to make "substantive progress towards political reforms to justify the resumption of aid".

In moving against Banda's regime, the donors followed a pattern set in November 1991 when all aid to Kenya was suspended for six months because of widespread corruption, economic mismanagement and the stifling of political dissent. By suspending aid to Malawi, the donors punished the government for its political practices.

The crucial fact about the withdrawal of Western aid concerns its devastating impact on the Malawian economy.

Aleke Banda described the impact of the donors' decision in a BBC interview in August 1992: "The economy is declining daily

because of the withdrawal of aid. There is a great deal of insolvency and salaries for teachers and nurses are not being paid. The university is closed because of lack of finances and the government has just added 20 tambala to a litre of petrol. Now we face another round of price increases."

Asked if it was right for Western donor countries to impose strict economic sanctions, Mr Banda replied: "Economic aid should be withheld until there is irreversible political change in Malawi."

The government decided to seek aid elsewhere. Mr Chimango told parliament during the 1993–94 budget speech that K425m of the K511.34m development budget would come from external sources, namely Japan, China and Taiwan.[7]

With the economy sliding further into chaos, Banda needed to regain the confidence of the donor countries. In a desperate attempt to lure the donors into resuming aid payments, he announced on 31 October 1992, a future referendum on multi-party democracy.[8]

Chapter 7
The Role of the Christian Churches

The Anglican Church and the Church of Scotland were quick to support the bishops' letter.

Only days after the letter was published the Archbishop of Canterbury, Dr George Carey wrote: "The concerns expressed in the Bishops' pastoral letter are shared by Christians of all demoninations."[1]

Reverend Christopher Wigglesworth, General Secretary of the Church of Scotland's World Mission Commission, was equally supportive. In a letter to the Malawi High Commissioner he stated: "On behalf of the Church of Scotland I am writing to express in the strongest terms our protest at the recent arrest, interrogation and detention of the Catholic bishops of Malawi."[2]

Mr Wigglesworth refuted Banda's allegations that the churches were divided: "It is not true that the Roman Catholic church is on bad terms with us: on the contrary, we have an excellent working relationship, especially in Scotland, and we regard such statements as offensive."[3]

Banda's status within the church was also challenged. "It is not correct to describe the Life President as an elder of the Church of Scotland in any meaningful sense. While ordination as an elder is for life, a person with that status is not properly regarded as an elder unless they are a member of a kirk session. Dr Banda has not been such a member for nearly fifty years."[4]

These remarks encouraged the bishops but it took three months before the Anglican and the CCAP Churches within Malawi publicly endorsed the bishops' letter.

"There was no internal objection to the letter," remarked Bishop Donald Arden. "No one knew what to do and so they waited for others to take the lead."

The two Anglican dioceses in Malawi left it to the Anglican bishops of the Province of Central Africa – a group which includes Zimbabwe, Zambia, Botswana and Malawi – to make a statement. But difficulties in getting people together meant that nothing was done or said.

It was not until 21 July that the Anglican priests of the diocese of southern Malawi made a public statement: "We are in solidarity with the bishops' pastoral letter and we shall continue to work together."[5]

The CCAP church – a national independent Presbyterian church and the second largest church in Malawi – is organised into three separate synods (Livingstonia, Blantyre and Nkoma). Since the 1920s the Church of Scotland has developed close links with Blantyre and Livingstonia Synods.

On a visit to Malawi in May 1992, a Church of Scotland representative, Reverend John Wilkie, discovered some of the reasons for the delayed CCAP response.

> Distance and communication is a problem and the Presbyterian system of church government makes decisions without a meeting being called almost impossible. Also there is no recognised committee which is entrusted under its constitution to speak for the church in such situations. In addition there is a particular problem over Nkoma Synod which covers the part of the country that is Dr Banda's home area. The Synod appears to be anxious to dissociate itself from any protest.[6]

Despite these difficulties, the leaders of Blantyre and Livingstonia Synods met Archbishop Chiona and offered their private support.

Individual CCAP ministers felt less inhibited and used their Sunday homilies to express support for the bishops' letter. Reverend Robert Rasmussen, an expatriate Presbyterian minister, used the parable of the good Samaritan (Luke 10:25–40) to make his comments "Some of our brothers in the Roman Catholic Church have directed a letter to their congregations, pointing out the presence of the victimised sufferers lying as it were half dead along the side of the road. They have called their fellow Christians simply to face the truth."[7]

Rev Longwe was arrested and imprisoned on several occasions for preaching about social justice. His first arrest on 26 April resulted from a sermon based on the biblical verse: "The godly have been swept from the land; not one upright man remains." (Amos 2:12)

After his release on 9 May, Rev Longwe expressed no regrets about his action: "The church had to rise up against the situation and has taken a very clear stand. I was arrested because I preached against social injustice."[8]

The first public CCAP statement came during the visit of the World Alliance of Reformed Churches (WARC) in early June 1992). The CCAP leaders of Blantyre and Livingstonia Synods together with the members of the WARC delegation wrote a letter to Banda. Entitled *The Nation of Malawi in Crisis: The Church's Concern*, it asked Banda "to ensure that issues first raised by the Catholic bishops in their pastoral letter will be followed by genuine reform."[9]

The CCAP ministers introduced the idea of a "broadly based commission" which would make specific proposals for political structural reform.

Surprisingly, Banda replied within days. "My ministers will be ready to receive a delegation of the representatives of this local church to discuss these concerns. I would urge you to encourage them to hold such discussions with my ministers as often as they need to."[10]

Mention of a possible dialogue had positive spin-offs for the pro-democracy movement. First, Banda had seen off the challenge of the Catholic bishops especially with the confusion created after the visit of the Papal envoy and the failure of the bishops to condemn Mgr John Roche's deportation in mid-April. A second pastoral letter intended for publication on Easter Sunday never materialised.[11]

The fading leadership role of the Catholic bishops made it necessary for some other group to continue the challenge against Banda's regime. The involvement of WARC was both timely and influential.

Second, by encouraging CCAP representatives to meet government ministers, Banda had inadvertently created a new pressure group which backed the bishops' social critique and added practical proposals for political change.

For the next two months several letters passed between WARC and the Office of the President and Cabinet. WARC insisted on wider representation: "WARC wishes to associate the Roman Catholic and Anglican church in any discussions which might take place with your ministers. ... It would be be abnormal for a church to act in isolation from its sister churches."[12]

This ecumenical spirit was new to Malawi. Dialogue between the various denominations before the bishops' letter was virtually non-existent except for the occasional religious service or committee meeting. By uniting behind a common cause, extra force and credibility was injected into their efforts.[13]

The government adopted delaying tactics. John Tembo, the Minister of State, dismissed WARC's request: "The inclusion of people from other institutions is a departure from the Life President's directive. I think it is important that we keep to the word and spirit of the directive."[14]

The desire to show solidarity with the Churches in Malawi resulted in the visit of a British ecumenical delegation to Malawi (July 18–25). The three-man delegation travelled throughout the country meeting the church leaders. Their 2000-word report, *Critical Time For Malawi*, confirmed that "although Dr Banda had invited the churches in Malawi to discuss their concerns this has not yet happened." The report referred to the Malawians' "near total mistrust of government statements".[15]

Frustrated in their attempts to meet government ministers, several church leaders, business people and lawyers held a number of secret meetings at Chilema training centre in the south. On 28 August 1992 they formed the Public Affairs Committee (PAC), a broad-based group of Malawians pressing for new democratic structures and respect for human rights.

In a letter to Banda, PAC re-emphasised the need for partnership and dialogue: "The world is changing and changing quickly. Almost all of Africa is now in the process of self examination concerning good governance. We feel these changes have affected us too. The most important factor for us in this process of change is to be in control of the change and not to be overtaken by events."[16]

PAC became a respected and influential pressure group. By the start of the referendum campaign in January 1993, the two main opposition parties, UDF and AFORD, had joined PAC.[17]

Chapter 8

The Referendum Process

Opposition groups grew impatient over government inactivity. PAC urged Banda to act: "In the absense of any relevant comment coming from the government, everybody has been left to speculate about the country's economic and political future. This is not constructive and is very dangerous."[1]

The main political groups	
MCP	Malawi Congress Party
UDF	United Democreatic Party
AFORD	Alliance for Democracy
PAC	Public Affairs Committee

In a suprise move, Banda declared on 18 October 1992 that a referendum would be held to decide whether the people wanted to retain the one-party state or embrace a multi-party democracy.

The next day Banda went on the offensive. Speaking to a group of farmers at State house in Lilongwe, he denounced those who misinterpreted his intentions: "The dissidents are already misleading the people and are not ashamed of telling lies. I called for a referendum to give my people the chance to show their support and commitment to me and the MCP party." Banda encouraged Malawians to avoid "the disunity and chaos of the multi-party form of government. You have had 28 years of stable government and steady economic growth. There would be no reason to change from the present system".[2]

PAC resented Banda's dismissive attitude towards pro-democracy campaigners who he labelled as "dissidents" and "confusionists". Banda classified outspoken priests as mere "misguided clerics". In a letter to Banda, PAC asked Banda "to make a public announcement that they would not be harrassed".[3]

Others viewed the referendum as just a side issue. "Malawians do not need to be asked if they want the right to choose a multi-party system," declared a UDF official. "We already have that right." Meanwhile, AFORD and UDF claimed increased support in the rural areas. They campaigned for the suspension of Article 4 of the Constitution which enshrined the status of the MCP as the sole legal party. This meant AFORD and UDF could only operate as pressure groups.

A United Nations advisory group arrived in Malawi from 15–21 November. Confident of success, Banda had invited them to offer advice about how to organise the referendum. They drew up a list of detailed recommendations: the creation of a referendum commission; the release of political prisoners; free access to the media; an adequate voter campaign with mid-June as a possible referendum date; the use of one ballot box and an invitation to international organisations to act as monitors.[4]

It took Banda six weeks to respond to the UN proposals. In a national radio broadcast on 31 December, he announced 15 March as the date for the referendum. Anticipating opposition protests, Banda explained why he opted for such a early date: "Many preparations have already been done, or have already been going on for some time. It is important that we should avoid unnecessary delays." Banda rejected UN requests for one ballot box and free access to the state-run radio station. But he did allow "advocates of multi-party" to hold public meetings "with the permission of the local police."[5]

	Referendum Timetable
18 Oct.	Banda announces a forthcoming referendum.
15–21 Nov.	UN technical team arrives.
31 Dec.	Banda announces 15 March as the referendum date.
12 Jan.	12-member referendum commission approved by Banda.
22–26 Jan.	UN Team returns.
	Under pressure, Banda extends the referendum date to 14 June.
5 Feb.	Referendum regulations released.
14 Feb.	Second bishops' letter *Choosing our Future*.
17–19 Feb.	PAC Conference on Malawi, Swanwick, Derbyshire.
14 June	The Referendum.
16 June	Results show 63.5% for multi-party.
17 June	Banda concedes defeat.
29 June	Suspension of Article 4; opposition parties are legally recognised.

AFORD rejected Banda's referendum date citing inadequate prepartion time for registration and voter education. The Malawi Action Committee (MAC) expressed concern over the use of multiple ballot boxes and that March was in the middle of the rainy season when "roads are impassable" and "the agricultural cycle is at its busiest". Asking the police for permission to hold rallies fuelled the opposition's mistrust of Banda: "The police are an extension of the MCP and as such are an interested party," an

AFORD official complained. "It will lead to delays and possible denials".[6]

Banda's refusal to comply with essential UN referendum regulations and his insistence on 15 March reflected his determination to manage the referendum process. The continued intimidation and arrest of pro-democracy supporters reinforced Banda's control of unfolding political developments.

A report by a group of British lawyers who visited Malawi in September 1992 exposed a widespread climate of fear: "We wish to emphasise that the emotion we encountered among the citizens at every level from villagers to government officials was fear." Asked about political arrests, Friday Makuta, the then Minister of Justice, told the delegation. "I've no idea how many detainees there are." The lawyers decried detention in Malawi as being "without warning, without explanation, without trial, without limit."[7]

On 20 December more than 200 peaceful demonstrators were arrested in Blanytre for planning a march in protest at the imprisonment of Chakufwa Chihana, the AFORD leader. They were charged with unlawful assembly and released on bail after five days.

Individuals were rounded up. Journalist Felix Mponda was imprisoned on 2 January for possessing copies of a new independent newspaper *The New Express*. Rev Longwe's Scottish wife, Alice, Chakala Chaziya, the AFORD vice chairman, and the UDF chairman, Bakili Muluzu, were all briefly detained. Arrests became less frequent after March 1993.

The 12-member referendum commission was approved by Banda on 12 January. Opposition groups complained it was "overloaded with pro-MCP supporters". One commission member, Fr Joseph Tenthani, was one of three priests who refused to read the bishops' letter and took a copy of it to the MCP headquarters in Lilongwe.

"For many this was a scandal," complained the Right Rev Tarsizizo Ziyaye, Bishop of Dedza. "When he was elected onto the commission, the bishops were not consulted and we wanted him to resign from it."

The UN team returned to Malawi in late January. Fearing a mass boycott of the referendum, they persuaded Banda to change the referendum date to 14 June but he refused to budge on the thorny issue of ballot boxes.

People looked to PAC for guidance. Inexperienced and ill-equipped to cope with Malawi's first referendum, PAC sought assistance from the Council of Churches for Britain and Ireland(CCBI). Because PAC represented such a wide body of opinion, the CCBI invited PAC representatives to a two-day conference in Swanwick, Derbyshire, to discuss a programme of action.[8]

Several topics were discussed: Human rights and education for democracy; strategies and tactics during the referendum and the lobbying of international bodies. CCBI delegates issued a statement expressing their "strong support for PAC in its unifying role as it seeks to secure rapid, tangible and irreversible progress towards a new political order".[9]

Two PAC members, travelled to Geneva to meet the UN commission on Human Rights. "Unless the Malawi government accepts UN recommendations, the referendum will not be free and fair," said Rev Longwe. He urged the UN commission to encourage Banda to adopt the use of one ballot box, allow free access to the media and create an independent referendum commission.[10]

Back in Malawi the referendum campaign was close to collapse over the government's use of scare tactics to win voters. "Everything is clearly orchestrated" said one missionary priest. "First the meeting with the traditional leaders and chiefs. They have been told they will be the first to be removed if the dissidents win. Then they move on to the village people and the schools."

A fortnight's sampling of the government-owned *Daily Times* revealed that 51 out of 55 articles on the referendum called openly for one-party rule.

"Many people had become cynical about the referendum," remarked Martin Hill from Amnesty International. "They saw how the government biased the whole system against the multi-party vote and wondered whether it was worth voting."

Apart from the referendum, the effects of a serious drought and the presence of more than 1 million Mozambican refugees in Malawi had drained the people of energy and resources.

In an attempt to stem the tide of apathy among local people, the Catholic bishops issued a second pastoral letter, *Choosing Our Future*. "We felt strongly that people needed to be guided about the referendum," said Bishop Zizaye."They had many unanswered questions."

The bishops decribed the referendum as "historic" and "a turning point" in Malawi's history" and encouraged the people to vote:

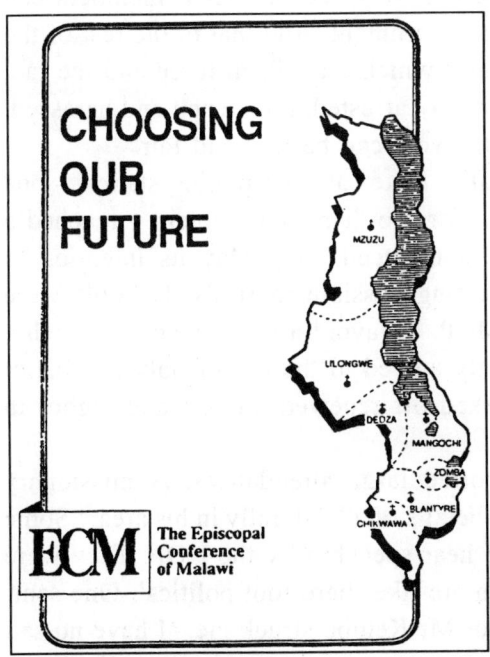

"Commitment to faith covers the whole of our lives especially our social, economic and political obligations."

They condemned government intimidation: "It is the basic right of people to make a choice, free from force, threats, fear and harassment."

The letter, read out in all Catholic churches on 14 February, analysed the advantages and disadvantages of single and multi-party political systems but stressed the bishops' neutrality: "The church does not advocate a particular party ... The Church does not and will not tell people how they are to vote." Despite attempts not to sway the voters, the bishops highlighted seven reasons in favour of multi-party politics compared with only three for a single party system.[11]

By May, both The Law Society of England and Wales and the human rights group Article 19, argued that the referendum would not be fair and free. Addressing the legal basis of the referendum regulations, the Law Society concluded: "They are flawed in certain aspects and are therefore not adequate." The phrasing of the referendum question on the voters slip was seen as "too long and unclear" and "not capable of being answered yes or no".[12]

Richard Carver, Article 19's Africa Research Coordinator, commented at the time: "The conditions for the campaign are simply not equal. Access to the radio is crucial. Opposition groups are not allowed to be interviewed by voice but MCP members can because they represent the government. Add that to the rest of the regulations like sedition laws which are still in force and the fact that people are being constantly arrested, threatened and harassed. It is difficult to see how the vote can be free and fair."[13]

The issue of the two ballot boxes at each polling station – one for the MCP and the other for pro-democracy voters – reached a peak in early May. PAC announced on 7 May its intention to boycott the referendum fearing possible reprisals if people were seen to vote against the MCP. To avoid a mass boycott at such a late stage, Banda reluctantly agreed to the use of only one ballot box and his decision sparked off renewed interest and vigour in the referendum campaign.

Opposition groups reported large attendances. A missionary priest in Balaka recounted details of a UDF rally in his area. "Some 8,000 people turned up to hear speeches by the UDF. They were not of 'high politics' but more like 'bare foot politics'. One sentence from the UDF speaker Mr Kembo struck me: 'I have no salt to give you, I don't have cars to promise or food to distribute. What I have brought is freedom.' In all its simplicity it was a miracle that it could have happened. But it will be important to give a content to terms like democracy, referendum and freedom."[14]

The rallies followed a similar pattern to the MCP meetings and led one journalist to ask: "Why are pressure groups copying MCP culture. I thought they were fighting for change, complete change ... So what do they want to change?"[15]

Dwindling support for the ruling MCP forced Banda to appear at MCP rallies. Worries over his increasing fragility surfaced at a political rally in Dedza. Exhausted after reading three pages of script, he sat down without reading the crucial anti multi-party section. As the crowd drifted away they were suddenly called back to hear Banda finish his prepared text.

Referendum day passed off smoothly with only a few minor snags. International observers were deployed in teams of 3–4 people. "Our team was sent to Chikwawa in the extreme south,"

Preparations for the referendum

5,326	polling stations
2,066	polling centres
4.700,000	voters to register
5,000,000	envelopes and voting papers
5,000	litres of indelible ink
35,000	identification badges
210	international observers
28	ecumenical observers

explained Rev Tony Cox, a member of the ecumenical observer team. "From around 5 a.m. until after midnight we visited polling stations. Our own group visited almost 20 stations, several of

Voters registered for referendum	4,699,527
Those who voted	3,153,448
Null and void votes	70,979
Votes for single party	1,088,473
Votes for multi party	1,993,996

The Referendum Commission 15 June 1993

them more than once. None of us failed to be moved by the long queues of hundreds lining up to vote as the sun rose and the man who said 'I have waited thirty years to vote. To wait another two hours is no problem.'"

Another international observer described the voting procedure. "At each station, there was a table with three polling officials. The first official checked the hand of the voter to make sure there were no ink stains on the right forefinger which would have indicated that the person had already voted. The voter's name was then marked off the registration book by the second polling official. The third official dipped the voter's finger in ink and gave the voter an envelope and two ballots, one for *Tambala* (cock – the symbol of the MCP party) and one for *Nyala* (lantern – the multi-party sign). The voter went to a curtained booth, selected the ballot

	Single party	Multi-party	Null
North	11%	88%	1%
Centre	65%	31%	3%
South	15%	83%	2%

and then left the booth and placed the envelope in the publicly displayed ballot box."[16]

A clear majority (63.5 per cent) voted for the introduction of multi-party politics. International observers endorsed the referendum result. One group, the Association of European Parliamentarians for Southern Africa (AWEPA), echoed a commonly-held view: "The referendum cannot be considered fully free and fair no matter how well run the actual poll was ... We conclude that a result giving a large majority for multi-party system reflects the will of the Malawian people ... We call for the government and opposition to sit down urgently and work out a transition to a multi-party system."[17]

Overwhelmimg support for the MCP in the central region (65%) did not surprise the opposition groups. The region is the home of Banda and Mr Tembo and contains most of the tobacco estates where PAC was not allowed to campaign. Bishop Arden argues that the influential Nkoma Synod, which follows the conservative Dutch Reform tradition of stressing "the powers that be are ordained by God" (Romans 13:1), was a significant factor.

Jubilant pro-democracy supporters took to the streets of Blantyre. "Convoys of cars and lorries flying yellow flags, the colour of the multi-party groups, paraded through the main street" and "gangs of young people were shouting, waving, chanting 'no more Banda'."[18]

"The President has put himself in a very difficult position," said a UDF spokesman. "He told the people that they were choosing between him and multi-party democracy. The vote means the people have no confidence in him. The rightful thing for him is to resign immediately."[19]

Banda conceded defeat. "I have accepted the referendum result, and the government will respect the wishes of the people." But he quashed any idea of quitting. "The suggestion that the MCP or I should resign to be replaced by an interim government is out of the question." And he hinted at a long drawn out process: "There

must be extensive consultations between the MCP and the new political parties."[20]

Banda recalled Parliament on 29 June and Article 4 of the Constitution – which outlawed opposition parties – was repealed. Banda had finally accepted the end of nearly 30 years of one-party dictatorship.

Initial euphoria was short-lived. The PAC proposed the formation of a National Executive Council (NEC) to act as a temporary Shadow Cabinet until the general election. The government shelved the idea and plans to form a constituent assembly to draw up a new constitution were postponed.

Western governments reacted cautiously to the result. Britain waited three months before resuming partial aid to the government.

Chapter 9

A Changed Climate

I returned to Malawi in September 1993 – 18 months after the bishops' letter. I recorded the changes I saw in an article (reprinted below) entitled 'Kindly Leave the Stage'

(*The Tablet*, 30 October 1993).

Previously tight-lipped about politics, Malawians now openly discuss the downfall of President Banda and the ruling MCP. After more than 30 years under Banda's one-party rule, the June referendum vote on 14 June in favour of multi-party politics has released a flood of repressed anger and frustration.

"They cheated us for so long," said a waiter in a Blantyre bar. "Banda's time is up and we want him out of the way." I heard similar statements wherever I went. A primary school teacher in Lilongwe angrily rebuked the government's handling of recent civil servant strikes. "They tell us they have no money," she said "and yet this year all the ministers got new Mercedes, all the MPs got new pick-up trucks and Banda got a new helicopter. They can't treat us like children any more."

Such outbursts were unthinkable only a year ago. The new found freedom of political expression is matched by the emergence of a flourishing press. Fifteen newspapers have appeared in the last six months. Admittedly some are no more than newsletters but they are sold out within an hour of reaching the streets.

Headlines such as "Government is shattered", "Life Presidency goes" and "MCP assisted Renamo rebels" are indicative of a strong anti-government campaign. Only two papers, *The Daily Times* and *The Guardian* support Banda and the MCP.

Human rights abuses committed in the past are being exposed. The mysterious death of three cabinet ministers in May 1983 has recently received extensive coverage in the newspapers. The ministers criticised a plan by Banda to install John Tembo, the current minister of State, as the new Prime Minister. The press accuses the government of killing them and makes frequent references to what they term "the Mwanza murders". (Mwanza is the area where their bodies were found).

In the June 14 referendum, more than 63 per cent of the people voted to end 29 years of MCP party rule. However, the two main opposition parties, UDF and AFORD, frequently trade insults in their rival newspapers.

Only 100 signatories are needed to form a new political party. Last month, the formation of the Malawi National Democratic Party (MNDP) brought the number of opposition parties to seven. The multiplication of parties worries Bishop Mathias Chimole of

Lilongwe: "I feel uneasy about the number of new parties. They are too divided and only sow confusion among the people."

A priest described to me how villagers in his parish had been disconcerted. They had thought that the multi-party referendum victory would create "immediate prosperity with new roads and new jobs" and would bring "plenty of money to their villages".

There are fears of a repeat of the Kenyan general election in December 1992 when the ruling Kenyan African Nationalist Party (KANU) won because the two opposition parties were so far apart.

A credible alternative leadership is also lacking. "There's no one we can look up to," said Archbishop James Chiona of Blantyre. "We need a leader who is not tainted with the past or with alleged corruption scandals."

Presidential hopefuls such as Bakili Muluzi, the UDF chairman, is constantly quizzed about past business ventures while Chakufwa Chihana, chairman of AFORD, has disappointed people by travelling in a large presidential-style convoy to political rallies. It smacks of Banda all over again.

The MCP has yet to nominate a presidential candidate. John Tembo, the Minister of State and Hetherwick Ntaba, the Health Minister are the frontrunners but both are unpopular. "The country is leaderless," one Balaka businessman complained to me. "Living in a vacuum is no good for business."

President Banda has made only one speech since his defeat in the June referendum. During a series of civil servant strikes last month, the government made no public statement and the opposition leaders issued none.

"Banda should have resigned after the referendum and made a dignified exit," said a former MCP councillor. At 94, the President is rarely seen in public. "He's a broken man," explained one UDF supporter. "But he has been deified and so it's difficult to get rid of him."

The Malawians I spoke to believe John Tembo is running the country and has been for years. One, a retired factory worker, echoed a common sentiment: "He's still there holding up the progress of democracy because he wants to stay on."

Meanwhile the Catholic Church enjoys popular support. The Catholic bishops' pastoral letter *Living our Faith* (March 1992) was seen by many as the turning point in the struggle for a more democratic Malawi. Another letter *Choosing our Future* (February 1993), explained the differences between retaining a one-party state or adopting a multi-party system.

Since then the bishops have remained silent. "We're not sure what to do now," said Bishop Alan Changwera of Zomba. "This is a totally new situation for us."

Archbishop Chiona insists the Church does not support one particular party but fears if the MCP gets back into power, "we will be back to where we started from". The neutrality of the Church is vital for aiding voter education on the forthcoming election. The Catholic press has printed more than half a million copies of a booklet entitled *What is democracy* and is preparing another one on the general election.

Although the confrontation with the government is less sharp, the bishops still fear for their safety. Bishop Chimole referred to a recent incident when the car of a fellow bishop was rammed and overturned. It caught fire and the bishop's driver was injured.

Archbishop Chiona had asked to be excused last month from attending the *ad limina* meeting in Rome because he thought it unsafe for all the bishops to leave the country.

The bishops are aware that freedom of political expression does not necessarily imply political progress. Banda and the ruling MCP are still in power and many Malawians fear that little has really changed.

Some hope was restored during September, however, with the agreement to ban the military wing of the Malawi Young Pioneeers (MYP); Banda dropped the title 'Life President'; the British government resumed partial aid to Malawi's development programme and the European Union promised to do the same if Malawi's human rights record improves.

Then at a meeting of the National Consultative Council (NCC) on 21 September in the capital, Lilongwe, it was agreed by the government and the opposition parties that Malawi's first general election would take place on 17 May.

Malawians must wait in uncertainity. But they know that political change is now irreversible, however long it takes.

Chapter 10

An Evaluation of the Bishops' Letter

The 'wind of change' – which had spread through South Africa, Namibia, Zimbabwe and Zambia – eventually reached Malawi in 1992.

Malawi had lost its special status among Western countries after the growth of the democracy movement in South Africa and when human rights began to play a factor in aid allocation. A small but effective underground movement wrote several unsigned letters urging political reform. Rampant government corruption, coupled with increased food prices and the effects of a severe drought intensified public resentment against Banda and the ruling MCP. Malawians were ready for change.

In March 1992 Malawi hit the international headlines. Up until then, press coverage was characterised by the occasional article which examined the whimsical nature of Africa's oldest head of State. The bishops' pastoral letter *Living Our Faith* (8 March) changed all that and sparked off a flood of articles about Banda's repressive regime.

The letter was the first public and detailed condemnation of extensive human rights abuses committed during Banda's 28-year dictatorship. It was a bold and dangerous move; exiled government critics had been killed for less dramatic outbursts. But the bishops' letter proved to be a decisive breakthrough and a catalyst for political change.

The letter came as a total surprise. The Catholic Church had remained silent over the mysterious death of three cabinet ministers in 1983 and the deportation of all Northern teachers from the South and Central regions in February 1989. The visit of Pope John Paul II in May 1989 seemed to cement ties between the Church and State, and only days before the letter, Archbishop Chiona publicly thanked Banda for being a "dynamic leader".

Government reaction to the letter proved as important as its content. Within days the government launched a frenzied campaign to prevent the bishops gaining support. The bishops were detained, the letter was labelled seditious, mass arrests were made and senior MCP officials plotted to kill the bishops.

Such actions prompted an unprecedented outpouring of public defiance; student marches in Blantyre and Zomba, strikes in the Central and Southern regions and the formation of opposition groups. It is unlikely that Chakufwa Chihana would have returned to promote multi-party democracy without such large-scale public demonstrations in support of the bishops.

Banda underestimated the influential international dimension of the Catholic church. The Pope sent his Papal Envoy, Archbishop Giovanni De Andrea, to secure the bishops' safety while 23 international episcopal conferences asked the European Union to intervene. Various Christian leaders from all over the world wrote letters of support.

Suspension of aid to Malawi can be linked to widespread international criticism of how the government reacted to the bishops' letter with mass arrests and a plot to kill them. The death of 38 people during riots in May 1992 finally prompted the Western donors to cancel all aid to the government – except humanitarian aid – until "the implementation of substantive progress towards political reform". The suspension – due to finish after six months – lasted for more than 18 months.

Expectations of imminent political change led Malawians to a new sense of freedom. Normally reticent about expressing opinions, Malawians threw caution aside and openly discussed the political situation. "The bishops have opened our throats" became a common refrain. Bishop Chimole believes the dramatic impact of the letter resulted from the bishops' accurate articulation of public feeling: "I did not write the letter; it was written a long time ago on the hearts of our people."

Attempts by the bishops to enter into dialogue with the government were blocked. However the bishops had accelerated the pace of political change. Within weeks of their letter, the two main opposition groups, UDF and AFORD, claimed widespread support throughout the country.

Differences among the bishops emerged over the publication of further critical statements. These divisions and a constant fear for their own safety, led to a climb-down from their earlier leadership role. Other Christian churches, namely the Presbyterians and Anglicans, took centre stage and continued the struggle. In August 1992, they helped to form PAC which campaigned for more government accountability and democratic reform.

Determined to regain international respect and financial support, Banda announced a referendum in June 1993 on multi-party democracy. With 63.5 per cent of people voting in favour of abandoning the one-party state, Banda conceded defeat. An amendment to Article 4 of the Constitution allowed the existence of opposition parties. Malawi was no longer a one-party state and the country's first multi-party election was set for 17 May.

Other factors were at work in the push towards political reform. Amnesty International chipped away at Banda's foreign image as an eccentric but benign leader. During the 1980s when Western leaders regarded Banda – the old man with the Homburg – as a reliable anti-communist, Amnesty revealed damning evidence against his totalitarian regime. In 1983 they exposed the killing of the three cabinet ministers and led a vigorous campaign for the release of political prisoners such as Jack Mapanje and Chakufwa Chihana.

Weekly reports of mass arrests and regular updates on the referendum and the general election process kept the international community informed of government attempts to thwart the democratic process.

The media, especially the BBC World Service, played its part. Before the government could react, the bishops' letter was broadcast to a potential audience of 120 million BBC World service listeners. The letter could no longer be treated as a mere domestic dispute. The government was forced to act cautiously.

"The BBC is important in countries where the media is less developed," argues Carolyn Dempster, Deputy Editor of BBC's *Network Africa*. "Our audience in Malawi is high because people do not trust the information of the government-run radio station. In fact they listen to the BBC to find out what is happening in their own country."

During a three-month period after the bishops' letter, the two main BBC World Service programmes for Africa, *Focus on Africa* and *Network Africa* broadcast more material on Malawi than in the whole of the previous three years. British newspaper coverage reached record levels with intense speculation that Africa's oldest dictator was about to fall.

Interviewed in September 1993, Archbishop Chiona, head of the Catholic church in Malawi spoke pessimistically about the Church's relationship with the State.

"As Catholic bishops, we find ourselves in a situation which amounts to our non-acceptability by the MCP." In order to avert a widening rift, Archbishop Chiona and the Minister of Home Affairs, Gwanda Chakuamba, met on 24 November and 1 December 1993 to discuss improving relationships.

Determined to effect a reconciliation, Mr Chakuamba arranged a meeting between Banda and the Archbishop on 3 December. On the same day a government press statement announced that "with immediate effect, the ban which was placed on the pastoral letter has been lifted and the deportation order served on Mgr Roche has been rescinded ... As a result relations between the government and church are back to normal."

Mgr Roche returned to Mzuzu diocese from where he was expelled in April 1992. "This is my place. This is where I should be," said Mgr Roche. But he expressed concern about his safety: "I've been advised not to travel alone." His last remark indicates that tensions still exist.

In January 1994 the Catholic bishops published a pastoral letter on *Caring for Our Families*. Catholics were keen for the bishops to address the issue of multi-party elections on 17 May. The bishops responded on 20 March with a 20-page pre-election pastoral letter, *Building Our Future*. More than 30,000 copies of the letter were printed in the yellow colour of the multi-party movement and it was widely circulated outside the Catholic Church.[1]

The bishops urged people to vote responsibly. "This is a critical moment in the history of Malawi. It is the beginning of a new political era ... The people will democratically choose for the first time a President and a government ... A good start can be made by electing only people of high integrity, men and women motivated by a desire to serve rather than a hunger for power."

As in previous pastoral letters, the bishops adopted a non-partisan approach. "As bishops we do not wish to enter into party politics. We have no intention of telling Christians which party or individual they should vote for. This is not our task."

The positive tone of the letter was mixed with apprehension about certain developments. "For a country to have too many political parties does not contribute to good government ... It is of great importance that journalists and others take great care to speak and write what is true and important. We invite all citizens to be more critical with regard to what they read and hear ... All forms of intimidation and harassment must be rejected by all the parties."

Fearing post-election violence, the bishops stressed the need to accept whoever wins. "There are sufficient examples from some other countries of long-term communal violence following general elections ... Such an outcome is to be scrupulously avoided."

The letter ended with words of hope: "We remember the past; we look to the future. Our dream is of better things and a better future; better for every person and for the whole community." That hope is shared by most Malawians despite the present reality of political and economic uncertainty.

Chapter 11
An Uncertain Future

Malawi is still in a delicate transitional period. Optimism about the democratic changes in Malawi is tempered with considerable political uncertainty as seen in the unexpected violent disarming of the MYP by the army in December 1993.

A damaging rift between the army and the MYP surfaced after the June 1993 referendum. Banda had deliberately kept the army small. This ruled out the possibility of a military coup and allowed him to increase the powers of the police and the MYP. But dwindling South African military support and commitment to protect the Nacala train route with Malawian soldiers forced Banda to increase the army from 5,250 in 1987 to more than 10,000 in 1993.

Meanwhile the MYP was seen as a private militia of the ruling MCP party which inflicted widespread intimidation on opposition supporters during the referendum campaign. Extensively armed and under the control of the Minister of State, John Tembo, the MYP became a real threat to the army. In September 1993, the MCP agreed that the 2,000 strong MYP be disarmed. This did not happen.

After the shooting of two soldiers in the Northern city of Mzuzu on 3 December, the army launched *Operation Bwezani* with the sole aim of disarming the MYP. Although the military operation was widely welcome, it proved to be a bloody affair. More than 30 people died. MYP buildings were burnt to the ground and the national MCP headquarters in Lilongwe was looted. Only the urban MYP centres were attacked, leaving hundreds of MYP in rural areas untouched. They fled into neighbouring Mozambique.

It was the first time since independence that the army had directly intervened in Malawi politics. No longer can it be seen as an ineffective force. The possibility of future military involvement looks likely. The Minister of Defence, Major General Mponela, insists the disarmament exercise is still on but hundreds of armed MYP are roaming freely in neighbouring Mozambique despite several meetings between the Malawian and Mozambican governments. The MYP remain a potential destabilising factor.

Political Reform

The government and PAC agreed in July 1993 to form the National Consultative Council (NCC) to oversee the transition from one-party rule to multi-party democracy. The NCC – similar to a shadow parliament – was asked to formulate policies and draft the new Constitution while a sub-committee, the National Executive Committee (NEC) – similar to a shadow cabinet – monitored their implementation.

The first major step towards constitutional reform was taken in November 1993 when the parliament enacted a programme of legal reform. Some oppressive provisions in Malawian Law were repealed: *The Forfeiture Act* which had allowed the government to seize the property of political dissidents; *Decency in Dress Act* under which men and women could be imprisoned and fined on account of their clothing or hair style. *The Preservation of Public Security Act* removed the government's powers of arbitrary detention.

The Penal Code Amendment Bill had the phrase "intention to incite violence" inserted as an essential element in the definition of "sedition" and not just "the expression of dissent"; *The Constitution Amendment Bill* introduced a limited bill of rights.

Some months earlier, the government had passed measures recommended by PAC and human rights groups such as a general amnesty for political prisoners; lifting the ban on the Jehovah's

Witnesses religious sect; allowing independent newspapers and magazines to publish; permitting independent human rights groups to be formed.

Certain laws were left untouched. The right to restrict freedom of expression by banning publications under at least three separate laws was retained. Laws such as *Censorship and Control of Entertainments Act* and several sections of *The Penal Code Act* remain in force.[1]

There is no television in Malawi and the one radio station is accused of bias towards the MCP. Amnesty International is keen to see "a substantial amendment of the *Malawi Broadcasting Corporation Act* in order that MBC becomes a genuinely independent broadcaster. At present the MBC is governed by a board which is appointed by and answerable to the Minister of Information and Tourism. Under section 17, he alone decides what is "contrary to public interest". MBC should also broadcast in other Malawian languages such as Tumbuka, Yao and Lomwe."[2]

The all-party NCC Conference met on 21–23 February 1994 to draft a new Constitution. It is not clear whether the country is to adopt a parliamentary mode of Constitution like the British one or the American presidential model.

Lack of agreement on constitutional changes worries Malawian lawyer, Modicai Msisha. "We need institutional safeguards to protect fundamental rights ... or that freedom we so fiercely fought and voted for may be handed over to more vigorous dictators."

Opposition Parties

The Kenyan election in December 1992 should have alerted the opposition to the danger of wallowing in the euphoria of their referendum victory before any substantive change had been achieved. Malawian author John Lwanda points to effective government tactics. "The failure of the pro-democracy elements to adopt their own agenda showed the paralysing extent of the one-

> **The Political Parties**
>
> Malawi Congress Party (MCP)
> Alliance for Democracy (AFORD)
> The United Democratic Front (UDF)
> The Malawi Democratic Party (MDP)
> The United Front for Multi-Party Democracy (UFMD)
> The Malawi National Democratic Party (MNDP)
> The Malawi Democratic Union (MDU)

party monolith created by Banda. Tembo just delayed with his usual mixture of 'respect for tradition and respect for his Excellency'."[3]

The opposition parties were criticised during the election campaign for not adequately addressing fundamental issues such as land entitlements, low incomes, unemployment, abuse of women, exploitative agricultural practices and unequal regional development. Some opposition leaders seemed more intent on getting into power and the existence of several parties improved the MCP's chances of retaining power. AFORD was singled out for being too regional while the UDF's 49-man shadow cabinet smacked at past MCP's extravagances.

All the parties wanted the MCP to lose but uniting them under one presidential candidate proved to be a controversial issue. While the UDF, MDP and UFMD expressed interest in the idea of unity, AFORD always rejected the idea.

AFORD's chairman, Chakufwa Chihana, and the UDF chairman, Bakili Muluzi, were the main opposition presidential contenders. But the UDF always had the edge since it was larger and better organised and enjoyed the support of the business community.

The MCP

Mudslinging and divisions among the other opposition parties helped the MCP to reconsolidate its power-base. The party strategy evolved around winning all or most of the parliamentary seats in the Central region – the home of Banda and Mr Tembo – and that a divided opposition would allow the MCP to win enough seats in the other regions.

MCP election rallies highlighted the party's record in office; it laid the infrastructure for health, education and social services, and maintained law and order with no ethnic upheavals. In contrast, multi-party politics only created chaos and division.

On 13 February the MCP named Banda as their Presidential candidate. A former detainee, Gwanda Chakuamba, was elected as his deputy and virtual successor. The party could not bring itself to relinquish Banda as a figurehead and he was chosen to take charge of the country – if only nominally – until the polls. Mr Chakuamba is the party's real choice for the future.[4]

Does this mean that the Minister of State, John Tembo – Banda's closest ally since independence – has decided to take a back seat?

He is deeply unpopular among the people and this may explain why senior MCP officials excluded him from the leadership race. He is too influential and ambitious to quit and is likely to enter the contest at a later stage. The new leader – whoever he is – cannot expect to receive the respect shown to Banda who at 94, is still honoured for bringing independence to Malawi.

Several MCP rallies addressed by Mr Chakuamba were disrupted. He was stoned at one rally in Bangwe on 3 January after criticising the opposition. Rumours abound as to who was behind the attack. Some pointed the finger at UDF supporters and others at those loyal to Mr Tembo. Some newspaper reports spoke of MCP voters being wooed with cash hand-outs and second-hand clothes.

An Uncertain Future

Past events still haunt the MCP. Senior MCP officials have refused calls for a Commission of Inquiry into the death of three cabinet ministers and one MP in a car accident at Mwanza in 1983. The Minister of Transport, Dr Hetherwick Ntaba, argues that "there is no new evidence to disprove the four died in a car accident". However, Machipisa Munthali, who was detained for 27 years at Mikuyu prison in Zomba, disagrees and has testified that the

Diary of Events

2 Oct.	Banda flown to South Africa for neuro-surgery.
15 Oct.	A three-man Presidential Council (PC) chaired by Gwanda is sworn in to run the country.
24 Oct.	Banda returns from Johannesburg.
16 Nov.	Parliament in Zomba repealed a number of repressive laws such as detention without trial and introduced a Bill of Rights.
3 Dec.	The army forcefully disarms the MYP in Lilongwe after two soldiers were killed on 1 December by MYP in Mzuzu.
6 Dec.	Banda resumes full Presidential powers. The PC is disbanded.
13 Feb.	Banda elected MCP's Presidential candidate with Gwanda Chakuamba as his deputy.
21–23 Feb.	NCC conference on drafting a new Constitution.
20 March	The bishops' third pastoral letter, *Building our Future*, is read out in all Catholic churches.
17 May	Malawi's first multi-party election.

cabinet ministers were detained overnight at the prison in May 1983. He said there were many eye witnesses apart from himself.

Even if the inquiry went ahead it is unlikely to unearth the truth. It seems the government has already destroyed sensitive security documents. A worker at the archives department in Zomba said: "We have identified documents to be destroyed. Some have been burnt and the exercise is still continuing. This is why the archives department remains closed to the public." The worker confirmed that the order to destroy the files had come from the Office of the President and Cabinet (OPC).

The MCP is constantly quizzed in the newspapers over lavish expenditure. One report described how in 1991 the MCP purchased a new presidential limousine for Banda at a cost over £250,000. He never used it. In the same year, cabinet ministers received new Mercedes which were replaced in 1993.[5]

The Press

The proliferation of uncensored newspapers – no fewer than 21 – is the most visible sign of change. Mostly they are four or eight page tabloids operating on a shoestring budget. Some of the reporting is speculative and inaccurate but most papers adopt a responsible and restrained approach.

It is still early days and the Journalists Association of Malawi (JAM) recognise their limitations. "We definitely are off to a bad start and have earned ourselves the name of 'opposition press' rather than the 'independent press'. When will we begin to explain the complexities of a pluralistic system of government?"[6]

An unprecedented level of criticism in the independent press is allowed.

There are frequent scathing attacks against the MCP. Reviewing 30 years of independence, an editorial in *The Monitor* concluded: "The best the government has achieved is to make Malawians brainless, thoughtless and spineless."[7]

A new breed of satirical cartoonists has emerged. A typical example is shown in the cartoon below. In 1990 Banda ordered old and ugly looking buildings in Blanytre to be marked with a red star. This meant they would be demolished if the owners failed to improve their outward appearance. The red star is now on Banda's head.

The new press is essentially an urban phenomenon. Only 10 per cent of Malawi's population lives in the towns and the newspapers seldom circulate outside Blantyre, Lilongwe, Mzuzu and Zomba. Besides, the adult literacy rate is low and Amnesty International estimates that "three quarters of the population has no access to the printed word".[8]

Operation Red Star

But an independent press could be one of the lasting benefits of a multi-party regime. If some of the papers survive it will serve to force the new government to behave in a more transparent and accountable way.

The Economy

Britain resumed partial aid on 18 September 1993 and by December 1993, the Consultative Group of Aid Donors to Malawi met in Paris and agreed to restore the non-humanitarian assistance which they had suspended in May 1992.[9]

Mushrooming media in Malawi

The resumption of aid suggested that considerable change had occurred. Mr Chihana, AFORD's chairman, disagreed with the donors' decision. "Unless the conditions upon which aid was frozen in Paris are fully met by the MCP and its government, aid resumption will not serve any purpose at all. The new Constitution is not in place and some oppressive laws are still intact."

The new government faces an uphill economic struggle. The severe drought of 1992 devastated the all important agricultural section, and resumption of aid will not match the levels of Cold War assistance. The people's misery will continue if the current projections on the impact of AIDS prove to be true. The government must also grapple with rampant unemployment, dwindling resources, poor housing, deforestation, inadequate schools and hospitals and a stagnant domestic economy.

Regionalism is another problem. The collapse of the one party-state could see Malawi being torn apart by ethnic and regional differences. It is not unimaginable to see a three-way split with AFORD in control of the north while the MCP claims power in the Central Region and the UDF takes the south.

Crime is on the increase. Desperate for food and money, Renamo bandits – who entered Malawi with the Mozambican refugees in 1990 – have sold their guns to Malawian criminals. Armed robberies are on the increase and such violence will threaten future investment.

Guns are to be found everywhere and the prospect of violent resistance to change has become a dreaded possibility. In February customs officials discovered a substantial quantity of arms on a KLM (Royal Dutch Airline) flight from Amsterdam via Dar es Salaam to Malawi. The arms were destined for the Agricultural Development and Marketing Corporation (ADMARC). But there was speculation that the weapons intercepted at Lilongwe airport were destined for the MYP via John Tembo, the Minister of State.[10]

Further industrial unrest is expected as the inflationary impact of floating the local currency in early February 1994 takes effect.

The Malawi kwacha is depreciating rapidly and retail prices for some food products have already risen by 25 per cent.

Malawi has come along way since March 1992. The country is no longer a one-party state. Safeguards are in place to prevent a repetition of blatant human rights abuses committed during Banda's reign. But there is still along way to travel on the road to democracy and Malawians face a long hard slog ahead.

Endnotes

Chapter 1: Background Information

1. *Third World Guide*, 1993/94, page 396.
2. *Europa Year Book*, 1993, page 672. Of an estimated total labour force of around 3 million people, less than half are in recorded wage employment. The average monthly salary is $35 but less for those working on tea and tabacco estates. Real per-capita recurrent expenditure is set to drop by 30% in 1994.

   Population growth of 3.7% per annum has put great pressure on the land. Almost all suitable land is under continous cultivation and deforestation is increasing.

   Health services are over-stretched. The World Health Organisation (WHO) set $1.25 per year as the bare minimum to maintain health care. But a report by the United Nations Development Programme (UNDP), *The 1993/94 Budget: What are the Priorities?*, page 4, April 1993, revealed that the 1993 budget allowed only 44 cents.

   Malawi has witnessed an alarming increase in AIDS: 20% of pregnant women have tested HIV positive and WHO estimates that 20% of the adult population are HIV positive.

   Enrolment for primary school is 42% with classroom ratios deteriorating to about one teacher to 65 pupils. A shortage of schools means that only 7% of those completing primary school gain admission to secondary school. Less than 1% enter university.
3. *World Bank Report 1993*.
4. Philip Short, *Banda*, page 85. Mr Short suggests 1898 instead of 1906 as the most likely date for Banda's birth.
5. Trevor Williams, *Malawi: the Politics of Despair*, page 176.
6. John Lwanda, in his book *Kamuzu Banda of Malawi, A Study in Promise, Power and Paralysis*, page 8, exposed striking contradictions in Banda's personality. "His north London patients adored him and still tell visiting Malawians what a great doctor he was ... Yet was it the saintly doctor or

the Banda of the Ghanaian vintage who practised abortions? The same doctor banned any public discussion of family planning in Malawi between 1964–1982."

"The shy Hastings Banda was to become the charismatic "ngwasi", "messiah" and "father and founder" of the nation to his supporters ... but countless others were later to find Banda an intimidating bully who detained thousands, apparently without mercy."

Banda's avowed puritanism versus his illicit relationship with Margaret French was another example of moral inconsistency.

7. Philip Short, *Banda*, page 202.
8. *Ibid.*, page 279.
9. Chris McGreal, *Esquire*, October 1992, page 132.
10. Philip Short, *Banda*, page 256.
11. There are suspicions that Banda wanted an unpopular deputy in order to secure his own position.
12. An Amnesty International report on *Malawi Prison Conditions*, February 1992, page 1, states that the government released 88 political detainees in the first half of 1991 and 22 in January 1992.
13. *The Daily Times*, Malawi, 30 November 1967.
14. *The Times*, London, 11 April 1987.
15. The *US State Department on Human Rights: Country Reports on Human Rights for 1992*, February 1993, page 152.
16. Legislative Assembly, 10 November 1965.
17. *Index on Censorship*, October 1989, page 32.
18. John Lwanda, *Kamuzu Banda of Malawi*, page 115.
19. Trevor Williams, *Malawi: The Politics of Despair*, page 262.
20. Frederick Pryor, *The Political Economy of Poverty, Equity and Growth: A Comparative Study of Malawi and Mozambique*, Oxford University Press, 1991, page 62.
21 *Ibid.*, page 13.
22 *Ibid.*, page 62.
23. *Third World Guide, 1993/94*, page 397.
24. F. Pryor, page 168.
25. *Ibid.*, page 147.
26. John Lwanda, *Kamuzu Banda of Malawi*, page 230.
27. *Europa Year Book, 1993*, page 673 and *Third World Guide, 1993/94*, page 397.
28. In 1915, Rev John Chilembwe, pastor of the Providence Industrial Mission

at Chiradzulo, led an uprising against British rule in Nyasaland. More than 200 rebels died in the conflict which lasted six days.
29. Catholic Institute for International Relations, (CIIR), *Malawi: Moment of truth*, London 1993, page 9.
30. *Statistical Yearbook of the Church*, Vatican Press, July 1993.
31. John Lwanda *Kamuzu Banda of Malawi*, page 26.
32. Letter from CHAM to Banda, 19 July 1993.
33. Africa Watch report, *Where Silence rules: The Supression of Dissent in Malawi*, October 1990, page 66. An article in *The Observer*, 11 April 1976, reported the incident of two Jehovah's Witnesses from Tembenu village who were denounced in January 1976 for refusing to buy MCP cards. They were brought before Kachoka, the local Youth League chairman. He had them tied up and beaten for three days. They were killed by having their genitals cut off. Kachoka was arrested but not brought to trial.

Chapter 2: Early Signs of Dissent

1. The ministers were Dick Matenje, Secretary General of MCP and Minister without Portfolio; Aaron Gadama, Minister for the Central region and leader of the House; John Twaibu Sangala, Minister of Health and David Chiwanga, member of Parliament for Chikwawa region. All four opposed a motion to amend the constitution so that the post of Prime Minister could be created. It was assumed that Mr Tembo was to fill the post.

   The killings came shortly after the assassination of another activist Attati Mpakati in Harare.
2. *Where Silence Rules: The Suppression of Dissent in Malawi*, October 1990, page 49.
3. *Where Silence Rules*, page 47.
4. *Where Silence Rules*, page 69.
5. *Network Africa*, 8 February 1992. This BBC World Service radio programme is transmitted to English-speaking Africa four times every weekday morning.
6. The group started in October 1991. Fear of infiltration meant membership was by invitation and meetings were arranged in different locations.
7. This coincided with the annual celebration of Martyrs' Day on 3 March.

Chapter 3: The Bishops' Letter

1. Six drafting committee members had responsibility for writing the letter. Mgr Roche did not write any part of the letter. Instead, he acted as co-ordinator.

2. Extracts from a press conference with Mgr Roche at the Catholic Communication Centre, London, 15 May 1992.
3. The ECM meets twice a year (January and June) at the Catholic Secretariat in Lilongwe. The bishops discuss matters relevant to the Catholic Church.
4. I am unable to reveal the names of the drafting committee in case of any future reprisals against them.
5. There are 130 parishes dotted around Malawi. Every parish has several smaller churches called outstations. Balaka, where I was based, had 21 outstations. Therefore, the letter was probably read out in over 1,000 churches. Three parishes in Lilongwe refused to read it.
6. Balaka press was started in 1988 by a group of Catholic Italian missionaries. It is a small venture with only one printing press, two computers, and a staff of four.
7. English is Malawi's official language even though only 10% of the people speak it.
8. The pastoral letter is printed in full at the back of this thesis.
9. MBC, 12 March 1992.
10. Originally, the meeting was due to be held at the Archbishop's house in Blantyre. The police changed the venue and indicated that the bishops could face charges.
11. Amnesty International lists "hundreds of people" who were arrested for possession of the letter. A woman office-worker detained in May 1992 for possession of the letter told a visiting delegation of British lawyers in September 1992 of her treatment at the hands of the police.

   "They said, 'You are in the hands of the government. We can do anything we like with your life.' Then they ripped off my clothes. They left me naked. They made me lie down. One pulled my legs. One man had pliers. They forced my legs apart. They started putting pliers into my anus. I was crying at the top of my voice." (Amnesty International report, *Preserving the one-party state*, 18 May 1993, page 2).
12. MBC, 12 March, 1 O'clock news.
13. *Malawi News*, 14 March 1992, page 6.
14. *Daily Times*, 13 March 1992, page 1.
15. *Malawi News*, 14 March 1992, page 1.
16. Malawi has two government-run newspapers, *The Daily Times*, a daily newspaper and *Malawi News* which appears on Saturday. However, in the past few months, a number of small independent newspapers have appeared – *The Financial Post, The Flame, The Mchiru Sun, The Nation, The Independent, The Monitor*.
17. Amnesty International, Urgent Action, no Afr 36/09/92, 20 March 1992.

18. According to local people, the MYP wanted to carry out a revenge attack on the press because the letter had been printed in their area. After the attack Fr Gamba was told by the police to leave the country for his own safety. He fled to Chipata in Zambia.
19. Extracts from three tapes which arrived in London in mid-April. Translated from Chichewa into English by Dr Jack Mapanje.
20. DCOP, Lilongwe Diocese, 22 March 1992.
21. Extract from a letter sent by the Archbishop of Canterbury, Dr George Carey, to Banda, 17 March 1992.
22. Church of Scotland press release, 16 March 1992.
23. Extract from a letter sent to US Secretary of State, James Baker, by Archbishop Daniel Pilarozyk, President of the US National Conference of Catholic bishops, 18 March 1992.
24. Western Donors' Paris meeting, 12 May 1992.
25. Nicholas Scott MP wrote to Baroness Chalker in response to an inquiry from one of his constituents, Mr Gerald Compton in Jersey.
26. European Parliament, resolution BB-0501-0538/92, 9 April 1992.
27. Ken Coates MEP wrote to Banda on 23 March 1992.
28. Between January 1991 and February 1992, *Network Africa*'s programme included only 4 packages on Malawi. From March 1992 to April 1993, 38 Malawi stories appeared on the programme.
29. The Independent (18), The Guardian (5), *Daily Telegraph* (4), and *The Scotsman* (2) carried the bulk of the articles.

Two articles in *The Observer*, 'Seized bishops free in Malawi' 15/3/92, and 'Malawi expels bishop during Easter service' 19/4/92, were sympathetic to the government.

Tiny Rowlands, chairman of Lonhro – owner of *The Observer* from 1981 to 1993 – had substantial business interests in Malawi. Julie Flint's article 'Land of the funny peculiar' (*The Observer*, 16/6/91) angered both Mr Rowlands and the Malawian authorities.

It contained a first-hand, impressionist account of a short visit to Malawi in which she mentioned how women can be imprisoned for up to six months for wearing trousers, and the banning of Simon and Garfunkel's song 'Cecilia' because it happens to be the same name as the official hostess, Mama Kadzamera. The government threatened to freeze Lonhro's assets.

In response *The Observer* printed a reply by Mr Tembo. His article, 'Malawi: Oasis of Achievement in Desert of Third World,' which appeared in *The Observer*, 29/6/91, included an abject apology: *"The Observer* regrets any errors contained in our report last week and is glad to give Mr Tembo this opportunity to reply."

This humiliating climb-down was not enough to satisfy the Malawi government and in the following week's edition, yet another apology was offered.

30. Mike Hall worked as a BBC reporter in Blantyre from October 1988 for 16 months – the first foreign correspondent to be based there since Philip Short in the 1960s. In February 1990 he was told to leave Malawi or he would be deported. Mr Hall was never told the reason and was given 48 hours to leave.

Chapter 4: Formation of Opposition Groups

1. Apart from Archbishop Chiona, Bishop Assolari and Bishop Chisendera (who was in South Africa receiving medical attention), the other bishops spent many nights sleeping at different parishes in their respective dioceses.

2. Chihana spent several years in a Malawi jail (1971–77) for campaigning in support of greater democracy in Malawi. Amnesty International's report *Fears for the safety of Trade Union leader*, 15 July 1992, stated that "during the seventies Mr Chihana was held in solitary confinement and ill-treated for long periods".

3. Mgr Roche insists the bishops' letter was primarily a pastoral document: "When we wrote the letter, we simply wanted, as pastors, to convey the Church's social teaching. Unfortunately, some people interpreted it in purely political terms."

    However, some statements were seen by the exiled opposition as an attack on the MCP and its policy of suppressing any form of political dialogue.

4. *The Malawi Democrat* was banned by the government in June 1992 but reappeared in October 1992.

5. There had been some confusion about the precise date of Chihana's release. AFORD announced 14 June but the High Court decided on 12 June 1993. Campaigning for the referendum ended (by law) at 6 a.m. on 12 June. Therefore, Chihana was prevented, not only from registering and voting in the referendum, but also from participating in any of the campaigning.

6. Until 29 June 1993, opposition parties were banned under Malawi's Constitution.

7. UDF resolved to condemn all acts of violence and intimidation by the government; to support wholeheartedly the Catholic bishops' letter; to ask the government to release all political prisoners, and allow the participation of other political parties in the political life of the country.

    A third opposition group, United Front for Multi-Party Democracy (UFMD), was formed in Zambia in January 1993. By August 1993, another two parties had joined the list of new opposition parties; The Mass Democratic Party (MDP) and the The Malawi National Democratic Party (MNDP).

8. There are more than 1 million northerners. They speak Tumbuku – their own tribal language. Generally they regard themselves as brighter and more industrious than the Chewa people in the centre and south of Malawi.

    Contempt for Banda reached a climax when, in February 1989, he ordered all northern primary and secondary teachers to return to their own areas because of alleged favouritism towards students from the north. In the referendum (14 June 1993), 97% of northerners voted for the introduction of multi-party democracy in Malawi.

9. Victory for the multi-party pressure groups in the 14 June referendum forced the government to change the Constitution on 28 June 1993, allowing the presence of opposition parties within the country.

Chapter 5: Factory Strikes

1. In the article 'Banda calls for calm after strikes', (*The Independent*, 9 May 1992, page 12), it was reported that the strike started when textile workers in Blantyre received a pay increase of 8% compared to the inflation rate of 16%.
2. *The Malawi Democrat*, Number 3, May 1992, page 2.
3. *The Independent*, 9 May 1992, page 12.
4. John Makina, a Field Officer with Action Aid, explained how his wife's monthly teaching salary rose from K169 to K312 after the wage increases in May 1992.

Chapter 6: Western Donors Cut Aid

1. *The Independent*, 7 June 1990.
2. *Where Silence Rules*, page 5.
3. *Malawi: Prison conditions, cruel punishment and detention without trial*, February 1992, page 1.
4. Mr Carver explained that it was beyond Amnesty International's mandate to call on governments to impose sanctions: "Aid donors put direct pressure on the government. We act on an informational basis."

    However, Mr Carver admitted that since 1988 Amnesty had used its special representative at the EC to expose the activities of the Malawian government.

    "The EC has been an important vehicle of pressure," Mr Carver said. "No doubt they have their own political reasons but they are usually sympathetic to allowing human rights a forum."

    The Western Donors' Consultative Group meets in Paris every two years to allocate aid to many third world countries.

5. In two previous Western donors' meetings held in Paris (1988 and 1990), Malawi received more than $500m.
6. *Washington Post*, 24 May 1992, page 3.
7. A report by the United Nations Development Programme (UNDP), *The 1993/94 Budget: What are the priorities?*, 23 April 1993, page 4, reveals that the government paid for increased spending on wages by cutting the budget for social services: "As a result, essential social and agricultural services will remain grossly underfunded during the fiscal year 1993/94."
8. Banda set 15 March 1993 as the referendum date. Due to opposition complaints about insufficient preparation time, the date was changed to 14 June 1993.

Chapter 7: The Role of the Christian Churches

1. Letter to President Banda from Archishop of Canterbury, George Carey, March 17, 1992.
2. Letter to President Banda from Christopher Wigglesworth, 16 March 1992.
3. *Ibid.*
4. *Ibid.*
5. Statement by the clergy of southern Malawi, 21 July 1992. The Anglican bishops did make a pastoral visit to Malawi from 21–25 September 1992. In a press release on 29 September they wrote: "The bishops were encouraged by the churches' resolute stand in upholding the cause of justice and playing a prophetic role at this momentous time in Malawi's history."
6. J. Wilkie, *Church and State in Malawi*, April/May 1992.

Rev Wilkie offers three possible reasons why Nkoma refused to support the bishops. First, the Synod covers Banda's homeland; second, many large tabacco and tea estates in the area were owned by the MCP elite and thirdly, the influence of the South African Dutch Reform Church which tends to separate church from state and emphasize a purely spiritual mission.

Banda rewarded Nkoma Synod's support for the MCP with a cheque for £40,000.

7. Part of a sermon given by Rev Rasmussen at St Michaels and All Saints church in Blantyre on 15 March 1992.
8. Extracts from a BBC interview on 13 June 1992.
9. Letter from WARC to President Banda, 2 June 1992.
10. Banda's reply to WARC, June 10 1992.
11. It is scarcely credible that the Vatican emissary who visited Malawi in early April 1992, Archbishop Giovanni de Andrea, would have been aware of the intended deportation of Mgr Roche. When he returned to Rome the Arch-

bishop declared that tensions between the Church and the Malawi government "were back to normal". So it must be supposed that he was deceived in the matter. Two other Catholic priests were also deported; Fr Patrick O'Malley (April) and Fr Tom Leaky (August).

12. Extracts from a letter written by Benjamin Masilo, Vice President of WARC, to President Banda, June 15, 1992.

13. The CCBI three-man ecumenical delegation which visisted Malawi from July 18–25 decribed in their report *Critical Time For Malawi* how the bishops' letter "brought the churches together in a new way. Anglicans and Presbyterians have told us how they were able to recognise the Catholic bishops as speaking for them. Clergy and lay people of the Anglican church and of the CCAP have expressed their whole-hearted support for the Catholic bishops. ... During recent months in Malawi, under the pressure of great national events, the leaders of the three historic Christian traditions have been finding themselves to be sisters and brothers in Christ in a quite new way."

14. A letter from John Tembo, Minister of State, to Rev Dr Silas Nyirenda, Senior Clerk for the CCAP Synod, 7 September 1992.

15. The three-man delegation included The Very Rev professor Bob Davidson, former Moderator of the General Assembley of the Church of Scotland; The Right Rev James O'Brien, Catholic bishop of Hertfordshire and the Right Rev Mark Santer, Anglican bishop of Birmingham. They were sent by the Council of Churches for Britain and Ireland (CCBI).

16. PAC's letter to Banda, 28 August, 1992.

17. The original name of the group – the National Affairs Committee (NAC) – was changed to the Public Affairs Committee (PAC) because the government disapproved of the word 'National'.

Chapter 8: The Referendum Process

1. An extract from PAC's letter to Banda, 28 August 1992.
2. *Malawi Times*, 26 October 1992.
3. PAC report *Mechanism of the Referendum*, 19 October 1992.
4. UN report on *The conduct of a Free and Fair Referendum on the Issue of a One-Party/Multi-party System in Malawi*, November 1992.
5. Extract from Banda's radio broadcast to the nation, 31 December 1992.
6. AFORD's statement on Referendum, 1 January 1993.
7. A Report *Human Rights in Malawi* by The Scottish Faculty of Advocates and the Law Society of England and Wales, 17–27 September 1992.
8. Set up in August 1992 to press for the democratic reform, PAC operated

as a non-partisan grouping of religious organizations, business interests and professional associations and as an umbrella organisation for AFORD and UDF.

9. Conference statement *Malawi in Crisis*, page 1,Swanwick, Derbyshire, 17–19 February. Conference delegates proposed a project budget of $520,000 towards voter education and arranged a meeting between PAC and David Steel MP, at the House of Commons.
10. Press Release, *Malawians speak to UN Commission on Human Rights*, Geneva, 25 February 1993. A Malawi special branch officer, spotted prowling the street of Swanwick, caused anxiety among some PAC representatives. No arrests were made on their return to Malawi but customs officers did confiscate large quanties of conference material.
11. The letter was printed in three langauages at Montfort Press in Balaka: Chichewa (16,000 copies), English (10,000) Tumbuka (5,000) and 30,000 copies of a leaflet *A Prayer for Malawi* were printed: "During this time we pray that the people of Malawi will be supported and inspired by our prayers and thoughts for the common goood. We also pray that justice, peace and truth will prevail in that country."
12. Report on *The Referendum on Malawi's Political System* by the British-Malawi Association of the General Council of the Bar, The Law Society of England and Wales and the Scottish Faculty of Advocates, 21 April 1993. The referendum question read: "Do you wish that Malawi remains with the one party system of government with the Malawi Congress Party (MCP) or do you wish that Malawi changes to the multi-party system of government." The lawyers felt the question carried the incorrect implication that a vote for the multi-party system was a vote against the MCP.
13. Article 19's report *The Referendum in Malawi: Free Expression Denied*, 27 April 1993, examined injustices committed by the government in the run up to the vote. The report spoke of opposition supporters being harassed, shot, arrested and denied direct access to the media.
14. The reference to salt is linked to opposition claims that MCP officials offered salt as a bribe to win voters.
15. *The New Express*, 27 April–3 March 1993.
16. Preliminary report on *Participation of the Ecumenical Observer Group*, 22 June 1993.
17. AWEPA's Interim report, 16 June 1993.
18. *The Independent*, 16 June 1993
19. *The Independent*, 17 June 1993.
20. Banda's radio broadcast to the nation on MBC, 17 June 1993.

Chapter 10: An Evaluation of the Bishops' Letter

1. Extracts from *Building Our Future*. The letter marked the anniversary of an earlier pastoral letter, *How to Build a Happy Nation*. It was published on 20 March 1961 and addressed Malawi's pre-independence problems.

Chapter 11: An Uncertain Future

1. Malawian law contained a large number of overlapping powers and this makes repeal difficult since it means several laws need to be repealed if all the loopholes are to be removed.

    The Parliamentary and Presidential Elections Act, passed in November 1993 guaranteed unhindered freedom of expression during the election campaign. However district commissioners and the police had to be notified in advance of any "campaigning" by the political parties. The law did not protect people who were harassed for wearing T-shirts with political slogans on them and for distributing party leaflets.

    The pattern of rural violence and intimidation which occurred in the months before the June 1993 referendum was repeated at least in the Central region. Opposition supporters in Dedza, Dowa and Mchinji reported cases of beatings and harassment by MCP supporters. In one incident a 14-year-old girl was beaten with bricks on her way home from an opposition meeting. And there was evidence that teachers were targeted by gangs because of their role in the registration of voters during the June 1993 referendum.

    A primary school teacher described the atmosphere surrounding the election as "calm but strange". "The opposition leaders accused each other and behind the scenes the MCP threatened village chiefs and civil servants particularly in the south."

2. Article 19, *Freedom of expression in Malawi*, February 1994.
3. John Lwanda, *Kamuzu Banda of Malawi*, page 315.
4. Mr Chakuamba joined the UDF after his release from prison in July 1993. He resigned a month later and rejoined the MCP. He rose quickly through the ranks, being elected Minister of Home Affairs on 11 September and then MCP Secretary General on 6 October. He had served 13 years of a 22-year prison sentence for uttering seditious words, unlawful possession of fire arms and possession of banned publications. At his peak Banda held four ministerial posts; Minister of Agriculture, External affairs, Works and Defence.
5. *The Weekly Mail*, 2 February 1994.

6. *The Review*, 24–30 January 1994.
7. *The Monitor*, 20 January 1994.
8. Amnesty International, *Malawi: A new future for human rights*, February 1994.
9. The British government agreed to provide Malawi with more than £10 million in balance of payments support. It was dependent on Malawi's adherence to the structural adjustment programme and its transition to multi-party democracy. Japan gave over 5 million pounds in debt relief and development.
10. Mr Tembo has been linked with Renamo and to the sending of hundreds of MYP supporters for military training to Renamo bases in Mozambique. Opposition sources contend that Mr Tembo wanted to employ these men in the run-up to the election or whenever he thought his authority was slipping.

    According to the General Makin Chigawa, Deputy Commander of the Malawi Army, some 500 armed MYP are still missing. This has fuelled speculation that they intend to return to disrupt Malawi's political progress.

Bibliography

BOOKS

Linden, Ian, *Catholics, Peasants and Chewa Resistance in Nyasaland 1889–1939* (Heinemann, London, 1974)

Lwanda, John, *Kamuzu Banda of Malawi. A Study in Promise, Power and Paralysis* (Dudu Nsomba Publications, Glasgow, 1993)

MacCracken, John, *Politics and Christianity in Malawi 1875–1940* (Cambridge University Press, 1977)

Mhone, Guy, *Malawi at the Crossroads* (Sapes Books, Harare, 1992)

Pryor, Frederick, *The Political Economy of Poverty, Equity and Growth. A World Bank Comparative Study of Malawi and Madagascar* (Oxford University Press, 1991)

Sanger, C, *Central African Emergency* (Heinemann, London, 1960)

Short, Philip *Banda* (Routledge and Kegan, London and Boston, 1974)

Williams, Trevor, *Malawi: The Politics of Despair* (Cornell University Press, London, 1978)

Europa Year Book 1993 (Europa Publications, UK, 1993)

REPORTS

Africa Watch	*Malawi: Deaths in Custody* (April 1990)
	Where Silence Rules: The Suppression of Dissent in Malawi (New York, Washington and London, October 1990)
Amnesty International	*Malawi: Prison Conditions, cruel punishment and detention without trial* (London, February 1992)
	Mass arrests of suspected government opponents (London, September 1992)
	Malawi: Preserving the One-Party State (London, March 1993)

Fears For The Safety of Pro-Democracy Activists (London, March 1993)

Human Rights Violations and the Referendum (27 April 1993)

Malawi: A New Future for Human Rights (February 1994)

CIIR   *Malawi: A Moment of Truth* (London, July 1993)

Law Society of England and Wales   *Human Rights in Malawi* (London, November 1992)

Article 19   *The Referendum in Malawi: Free Expression Denied* (London, April 1993)

Freedom of Expression in Malawi: More Change Needed (London, February 1994)

UN Development Programme   *The 1993/94 Budget: What Are The Priorities?* (Lilongwe, April 1993)

UN Report   *UN Technical team on the Conduct of a Free and Fair referendum on the Issue of a One Party/Multi-Party System in Malawi* (15–21 November, 1992)

MAGAZINES

The Economist   The Battle of Hastings, 21 March 1992
Malawi Elastic Banda, 24 October 1992
Into Africa, 22 May 1992

The New Stateman   Silenced Spring, 17 April 1992

West Africa   Malawi Human Rights abuses, 31 August–4 September
Malawi: Chihana heads new democracy group, 28 September–4 October 1992
Malawi Opposition Boycott, 29 March–4 April 1993
Malawi Economy declines, 12–18 April 1993
Malawi: One party rule ends, 21–27 June 1993

Africa Confidential   Malawi The Next Domino, 20 December 1991
Malawi: Western Notice, 8 May 1992
Malawi: Never the same again, 22 May 1992
Malawi: Referring to the opposition, 6 November 1992

Index on Censorship   Life Censor Banda, October 1989

In the Land of the Zombies, September 1991
The Press in Central and Southern Africa, March 1992
Thoughts for New Martyrs, May 1992

UK PRESS

Financial Times Malawi gets ready for life without Banda, 16 October 1993
Malawi troops attack military wing of party, 4 December 1993
Banda's nomination threatens reforms, 15 February 1994

The Guardian Fear of repression stalks townships of Malawi, 15 June, 1992
Caring Banda calls for calm after 40 die in riots, 9 May, 1992
Hundreds detained in Malawi sweep, 3 September, 1992
Malawi death clue, 30 October, 1992
Malawi legalises violence, 28 April, 1993
Banda's agents mount campaign of terror, 10 May 1993
Malawi cities reject Banda, 15 June, 1993
Banda faces demands for power sharing, 19 June 1993
Malawian opposition opts for joint control, 23 June 1993
Banda's operation leaves politics in disarray, 26 October 1993
Malawian troops take revenge on youth militia, 4 December 1993

The Independent Two traditions, a singular tragedy, 8 April, 1992
Malawi in grip of 'First Family' of fear, 12 April, 1992
West blocks aid to Malawi, 14 May, 1992
Banda meets church leaders, 6 June, 1992
Banda 'may start reforms', 1 July 1992
Lawyers fear for dissident, 16 July, 1992
Malawi police arrest clerics, 31 July 1992
Ministers threatened Malawi bishops, 10 October, 1992
Banda totters into step with the times, 30 October, 1992
Malawi opposition comes into the open, 12 December, 1992
Opposition holds rally in Malawi, 12 January, 1993
Opposition threat to boycott Malawi poll, 10 March, 1993
Gun fire at Chihana appeal hearing, 12 March 1993
Last African Dictator defeated by democracy, 16 June, 1993

	Banda lies low after Poll defeat, 17 June, 1993
	Let the people have their say in Malawi, 16 June, 1993
	Banda accepts deal on transition, 26 June, 1993
	Banda's return upsets Malawi, 8 December 1993
Daily Telegraph	Policemen stoned in Malawi riot, 9 May, 1992
	Malawi tea workers in pay strike, 13 May, 1992
	Opposition offers Banda dignity in defeat, 16 June, 1993
The Observer	Land of the Funny Peculiar, 16 June, 1991
	Malawi: Oasis of achievement in desert of third world, 26 June, 1991
	West may cut off aid after Malawi unrest, 12 April, 1992
	Malawi expels bishop during Easter service, 19 April, 1992

MALAWI PRESS

The Chronicle	Muluzi 'sure' of being President, 25 January 1994
	Government suspends loans, 1 February 1994
Daily Times	Party condemns Catholic bishops, 13 March 1992
	Malawi bishops are hypocrites, 26 March 1992
	Pastoral issue now resolved, 4 April 1992
	Government critic arrested, 8 April 1992
	Malawi refutes false allegations, 10 April 1992
	Surrender seditious letters, 4 May 1992
	Violence does not pay, 15 May 1992
	State, Church in Partnership, 25 May 1992
	Polling over, Nation awaits result, 29 June 1992
	Shocking news from Mzuzu, 1 September 1992
	Chihana to apear in court, 10 September 1992
	Referendum does not mean yes to multi-party, 26 October 1992
	Vote for black cock, 10 June 1993.
The Enquirer	MCP in Crisis, 2 February 1994
Financial Post	MCP licks its wounds, July 1993
Financial Observer	Voters confused over politics, 1 September 1993
The Guardian	Church–State not Rivals, 3–9 September 1993

Bibliography

The Independent	New Critique of the Malawi Constitution, 10–16 July 1993
	Mwanza road accident saga, 11–17 September 1993
	Malawi's political puzzle, 25–31 January 1994
Malawi News	Editorial: No mercy, 14–21 March 1992
	Incitements will not work, April 11 1992
	Chihana is a nobody to Malawians, 18 April 1992
	Police warning, 9 May 1992
	Editorial: Multi-party only brings confusion, 16–22 May 1992
	Two men set free from sedition case, 10 October 1992
Malawi Democrat	Plot to kill the bishops, 8 October 1993
	MCP declares John Tembo 'A clean innocent angel' 28 January
Michiru Sun	Road to multi-party politics, 16 July 1993
	Minister writes on Mwanza 'accident', 21 January 1994
	UDF ahead of the pack, 28 January 1994
The Monitor	The last dance, 9 July 1993
	MCP veterans face problems, 14 July 1993
	Religious leaders free to criticise, 2 August 1993
	MCP assisted Renamo, 6 September 1993
	Thirty traumatic years under MCP, 20 January 1994
The Nation	Building a democratic Malawi, 2 August 1993
	At last a truce, 16 August 1993
	Our country in transition, 24 January 1994
The New Express	Opposition watch out, 9–15 July 1993
The New Voice	Multi-party talks lose direction, 13-19 September 1993
	Press versus press, 24-30 January 1994
	We'll strip you naked, 24-30 January 1994
UDF News	Life Presidency goes, 1 September 1993
Weekly Mail	Kamuzu must retire, 13 January 1994
	Who inherits Banda's millions, 19 January 1994
	Banda still a candidate, 2 February 1994

Pastoral Letter

The Catholic Bishops speak out

Pastoral Letter from the Catholic bishops in Malawi. To be read in every Catholic Church on Sunday 8 March 1992 (the first Sunday of Lent). All bishops will be in their respective Cathedrals on this day.

Dear Brothers and Sisters in Christ,

As we commence this time of the Lord's favour, we, your bishops, greet you in the name of Our Lord and Saviour, Jesus Christ.

INTRODUCTION

As a community journeying in faith and hope, we recognise and accept the Lord's invitation proclaimed again in this time of Lent. On Ash Wednesday, we receive ashes with the prayer, 'Repent and believe the Good News'. This prayer introduces the period of Lent when we shall enter once more into the saving mysteries of the Lord's death and resurrection.

Christ began his public ministry by proclaiming: 'Repent and believe the Gospel' (*Mk* 1.15). In this proclamation he states the programme of his ministry: to call all humankind, in and through His life, death and resurrection, to conversion and witness. People in every age and culture are called to this conversion and to respond in commitment and faith.

In this conviction, we, your leaders in the faith, come to share with you what this faith invites us to as a church in the Malawi of today. We place this exhortation under the guidance of the Holy Spirit and the patronage of Mary, Queen of Malawi and of Africa.

1. THE DIGNITY AND UNITY OF HUMANKIND

Man and woman, created in the image of likeness of God (*Gen.*

1.26), carry in themselves the breath of divine life. Each created person is in communion with God. He or she is 'sacred', enjoying the personal protection of God. Human life is inviolable since it is from God, and all human beings are one, springing as they do from a single father, Adam, and a single mother, Eve, 'the mother of all those who live' (*Gen.* 3.20).

The unity and dignity of the human race have been definitively sealed in Christ the Son of God who died for us all, to unite everyone in one Body. Rejoicing in this truth, we proclaim the dignity of every person, the right of each one to freedom and respect. This oneness of the human race also implies equality and the same basic rights for all. These must be solemnly respected and inculcated in every culture, every constitution and every social system.

2. THE CHURCH AND SOCIETY

Because the Church exists in this world it must communicate its understanding of the meaning of human life and of society. As Pope Paul VI says, 'the Church is certainly not willing to restrict her action only to the religious field and disassociate herself from man's temporal problems (*The Evangelization of Peoples*, No. 34).

In this context, we joyfully acclaim the progress which has taken place in our country, thanks in great part to the climate of peace and stability which we enjoy. We would, however, fail in our role as religious leaders if we kept silent on areas of concern.

3. THE ASPIRATION TO GREATER EQUALITY AND UNITY

In our society, we are aware of a growing gap between the rich and the poor with regard to expectations, living standards and development. Many people still live in circumstances which are hardly compatible with their dignity as sons and daughters of God. Their life is a struggle for survival. At the same time, a minority enjoys the fruits of development and can afford to live in luxury and wealth. We appeal for a more just and equal distribution of the nation's wealth.

Though many basic goods and materials are available, they are beyond the means of many of our people. One of the reasons for this is the deplorable wage structure which exists. For many, the wages they receive are grossly inadequate, *e.g.* employees in some estates, some domestic workers, brick-makers etc. and this leads to anger, frustration and hopelessness. Another example of glaring injustice is the price paid to producers, especially farmers, for some of their crops. We wish to state that every person has a right to a just reward for work done, a wage which will ensure a dignified living for his or her family.

Not only has the worker a right to be paid justly by his employer, but he also has a duty honestly and responsibly to do the work for which he is employed. We would like to remind all Christian workers that their first duty on receiving their earnings is to look to the adequate support of their family. All too often workers spend their salaries for selfish purposes.

Bribery and nepotism are growing in political, economic and social life. This causes violence and harm to the spirit of our people. Honesty, righteousness, respect, equal opportunity for all: these must be the qualities which guide our nation as it grows and develops into the future.

One of the cornerstones of the nation is 'unity'. This reflects the will of our Creator that we live in mutual respect and oneness. Tribalism, apartheid (whether economic or social), regionalism and divisions are contrary to the call and truth of humankind. We call all the faithful to celebrate our common birth and destiny in mutual respect, acceptance, justice and love.

4. THE RIGHT TO AN ADEQUATE EDUCATION

A society which values its future affords the highest priority to providing education for all its young people. As it is commonly put, 'Young people are the future of the nation'. A sound education will aim at the following:

(i) creating an environment favourable to the physical, emotional, intellectual, relational and spiritual development of pupils;

(ii) developing in each student a respect for others and a recognition of civic responsibilities;

(iii) promoting the creative potential of students. The unique and diverse talents of every individual are recognised and encouraged;

(iv) instilling an appreciation of the students' cultural heritage, i.e. the linguistic, musical and artistic legacy inherited from the past;

(v) providing the students with appropriate training and skills which will equip them to make a living in the actual circumstances of our country;

(vi) seeking excellence, while aiming to provide education for everyone.

5. PROBLEMS OF OUR EDUCATION SYSTEM

At the outset, we wish to record how greatly we esteem and applaud the efforts which have been made by the government to provide education at all levels. The work of the Churches in this field has also contributed greatly to the advancement of our people.

Nevertheless we feel it necessary to draw attention to some of the problems which beset out educational institutions at present:

(a) Illiteracy

Illiteracy is one of the principal causes of poverty and lack of development. It cannot be said that we have succeeded in promoting the creative potential of our citizens while there remains a large scale problem of illiteracy in our society. It must be recognised that this is a problem which cannot be solved by state initiatives alone. Since a great responsibility lies with parents, we urge them to recognise this duty by sending their children to school.

(b) Falling Standards, Overcrowding and Shortage of Teachers and Materials

It is more and more widely recognised that standards of education are not only not rising, but are actually falling. Clearly there can be little hope of creating an environment favourable to the emotional, intellectual and spiritual development of pupils when schools are grossly overcrowded and suffer from a serious lack of teachers. While the present acute shortage has been made worse by the policy of requiring all teachers to remain in their own regions, final solutions to these problems will also demand generous increases in the resources made available to education. This will have very practical implications for the way in which our national priorities are established and the budget distributed.

(c) Unequal Access to Education

The criteria used in selection of pupils for secondary schools and third-level institutions should be known to all and be seen to operate fairly. Nor should they work to the disadvantage of particular individuals or groups. Access to education should not depend on whom the candidate knows nor how much money he possesses.

(d) Discipline

We believe that indiscipline is a major problem in secondary schools. It will not be solved by threats of punishments. There is a need to examine the underlying reasons for this state of affairs. Among them are:
(i) failure of parents to exercise their responsibility towards their children as they grow older;
(ii) lack of co-operation between parents and school authorities;
(iii) frustration due to poor or uncertain job opportunities;
(iv) manipulation of the selection process to include undeserving students;
(v) lack of support from higher authorities when action has been taken, or needs to be taken, by the school.

6. CHURCH–STATE PARTNERSHIP IN EDUCATION

Improvements will come about in the educational system only if there is mutual trust and genuine partnership between the different interested groups in society, *i.e.* parents, teachers, the Church and the State. In particular, we recognise the importance of Church–State participation in this area. On the one hand, the Church has a responsibility to support in every way possible the educational goals of the government. On the other, the government has a duty to respect the rights and legitimate aspirations of the Churches. Only through such a mutual recognition of rights and responsibilities will a fruitful partnership between Church and State be realised in practice.

7. ADEQUATE HEALTH SERVICES FOR ALL

Equality among citizens and the demands of justice call for policies which aim to provide adequate health care for all without distinction. The following principles have always guided us in this vital area of concern.
(i) Life is sacred. It is a gift from God to be valued from the moment of conception until death.
(ii) Human beings can never be reduced to the status of objects. We recognise that our bodies are temples of the Holy Spirit.
(iii) Every person is of equal dignity. The value of life is not to be measured by one's age,

possessions or position in society.

8. DIFFICULTIES EXPERIENCED IN OUR HEALTH SERVICES

We wish to pay tribute to the achievements of the government of Malawi in extending health services with the aim of providing the best possible care for all. Particularly worthy of mention has been the establishment of an excellent system of primary health care. The notable contribution of the Churches through their extensive network of hospitals and health centres is deserving of special praise.

At the same time, we are aware of the severe difficulties which the health services are experiencing at present.

(a) Overcrowding and Lack of Personnel

Without doubt, the most serious problem is the acute shortage of health centres to cater for the population. One cannot claim to uphold the principle of the sanctity of life if provision has not been made for even minimal health care for every person. This is a priority which a society cannot ignore if it wishes to be a caring and compassionate community. It must be recognised that if this problem is to be tackled, it will demand the allocation of more resources from the State.

(b) The Vocation of Caring for the Sick

Caring for the sick is a calling from God of a special dignity and importance. It can never been seen as just another job or another way of earning one's living. While we greatly value the generous dedication to service of many of those who work in the medical field, we cannot ignore that the quality of medical care is often seriously inadequate, *e.g.* patients being unattended to for long periods of time; the lack of commitment on the part of some personnel; the failure to recognise each patient as one's brother or sister in need etc. We therefore invite all health workers to serve every patient without exception with responsibility and true dedication.

(c) Inequality in Medical Treatment

Absolute equality of access to health care for all citizens is difficult to achieve. However, this is an ideal which must always be striven for. The guiding principle determining whether a patient will receive priority treatment ought not to be his apparent usefulness or his position in society. Rather, every person, whether rich or poor, educated or not, blood relative or not, has equal right to receive health care. The practice of stealing and re-selling medicines seriously threatens this right.

9. THE TRAGEDY OF AIDS

It is heartening to note the extensive health education programmes currently in operation in the state. One cannot fail to stress the importance of preventive measures particularly in respect of contagious diseases. The current epidemic of AIDS is a case in point. All recognise that in the present circumstances where no cure for AIDS is available, prevention in the form of health education is the only way of combating this problem.

We want to encourage the efforts undertaken in that direction and hope they can still be intensified: true facts about the disease should be made public more readily; information made available to all; personnel and resources freed for the treatment and counselling of the victims and their families.

However, preventive methods must respect God's law and enhance the dignity of the human person. It is most regrettable that little attention is paid to the fact that faithfulness to the Gospel's teaching on conjugal fidelity is the single most effective method of preventing the spread of tragic illness. We strongly object to the view that use of condoms is the remedy against this epidemic.

Besides the immorality involved in the indiscriminate distribution and use of condoms, we must be aware how much they contribute to spreading a false sense of security and encouraging a promiscuity which can only aggravate the existing problem. We appeal to Christian parents to protect and counsel their children against such practices and to guide them to true Christian understanding of sexuality.

10. PARTICIPATION OF ALL IN PUBLIC LIFE

In their writings to the Christians, both the apostles Peter and Paul note how the Holy Spirit grants the members of the Christian community gifts of all sorts for the benefit of the community. 'On each one of us God's favour has been bestowed in whatever way Christ has allocated it. To some his gift was that they should be apostles; to some prophets; to some evangelists; to some pastors and teachers.' Whatever the gift, the purpose is one 'to knit God's holy people together for the work of service to build up the Body of Christ'. (*Eph.* 4.7–16, *cf. Pet.* 4, 10–11).

African society has traditionally recognised that what is true of the Church is also true of any society; its strength resides in recognising the gifts of all and in allowing these gifts to flourish and be used for the building up of the community. '*Muta umodzi susenza denga*' [One head cannot carry a roof]. No one person can claim to have a monopoly of truth and wisdom. No individual – or group of individuals – can pretend to have all the resources to guarantee the progress of a nation. '*Mtsinje wopanda miyala susunga madzi*' [A river without rocks does not hold water]. The contribution of the most humble members is often necessary for the good running of a group. '*Wopusa anaomba ng'oma wochenjera nabvina*' [The fool beat the drum to which the clever one danced].

11. FREEDOM OF EXPRESSION AND ASSOCIATION

Moreover, human persons are honoured – and this honour is due to them – whenever they are allowed to search freely for the truth, to voice their opinions and be heard, to engage in creative service of the community in all liberty within the associations of their own choice. Nobody should ever have to suffer reprisals for honestly expressing and living up to their convictions: intellectual, religious or political.

We can only regret that this is not always the case in our country. We can be grateful that freedom of worship is respected: the same freedom does not exist when it comes to translating faith into daily life. Academic freedom is seriously restricted; exposing injustices can be considered a betrayal; revealing some evils of our society is seen as slandering the country; monopoly of mass media and censorship prevent the expression of dissenting views; some people have paid dearly for their political opinions; access to public places like markets, hospitals, bus depots etc. is frequently denied to those who cannot produce a party card; forced donations have become a way of life.

This is most regrettable. It creates an atmosphere of resentment among the citizens. It breeds a climate of mistrust and fear. This fear of harassment and mutual suspicion generates a society in which the talents of many lie unused and in which there is little room for initiative.

12. FOSTERING PARTICIPATION

We urgently call each one of you to respond to this state of affairs and work towards a change of climate. Participation in the life of the country is not only a right; it is also a duty that each Christian should be proud to assume and exercise responsibly. People in positions of authority, in government and administration, have a particular duty to work for the restoration of a climate of trust and openness. However, participation will remain a fiction without the existence of adequate channels of expression and action; and independent press, open forums of discussion, free association of citizens for social and political purposes, and the like ...

13. 'THE TRUTH WILL SET YOU FREE'

A first step in the restoration of the climate of confidence may be taken by recognising the true state of the nation. 'The truth will set you free' (*Jn* 8, 32). These words of Christ do not have an exclusively religious meaning. They also express a deep human reality.

For too long we have refused to see that, besides the praiseworthy achievement of the last decades, our country still suffers from many evils; economic and social progress does not trickle down to the mass of the people; much still remains to be achieved to make adequate education and health services available to all; the AIDS problem presents an incredible challenge; recurrent unfavourable climatic conditions often account for poor crops and subsequent misery for the people ...

People will not be scandalised to hear these things; they know them. They will only be grateful that their true needs are recognised and that efforts are made to answer them. Feeding them with slogans and half-truths – or untruths! – only increases their cynicism and their mistrust of government representatives. It gives rise to a culture of rumour-mongering. Real progress can only be attained when the true problems and the real needs are identified and all resources are channelled towards solving them.

14. A SYSTEM OF JUSTICE WHICH WORKS FAIRLY

We would like to draw your attention to another area of life in our society. We cannot ignore or turn a blind eye to our people's experience of unfairness and injustice, for example, those who, losing their land without fair compensation, are deprived of their livelihood, or those of our brothers and sisters who are imprisoned without knowing when their cases will be heard.

In a just society, a citizen must have easy access to an independent and impartial court of justice whenever his rights are threatened or violated. In particular, before a penalty is imposed, it is in the interest of justice and human dignity that the accused be informed in good time of the charge against him and be granted opportunity for a fair trial and, where necessary, the possibility of legal counsel. We call upon all and particularly those responsible for the administration of justice to ensure not only that procedures are respected but also that impartial judgement is rendered to the accused person. This will only be possible if the administration of justice is independent of external influence, political or other. Our bond of brotherhood and sisterhood in the one body of Christ and our solidarity as a people should not, in love, compel us to hunger for the justice and righteousness of the Lord in our society. In this context, we recall the words of Jesus at the beginning of his ministry: 'The Spirit of the Lord is on me, for he has appointed me to bring the good news to the afflicted. He has sent me to proclaim liberty to captives, sight to the blind, to let the oppressed go free, and to proclaim a year of favour from the Lord'. (*Luke* 4, 18–19)

This appeal for fair treatment should also be heard within the Church. We want to recall the importance of adhering to procedures which have been instituted to promote justice and protect the rights of the faithful. Our Church communities do need well-established and competent forums for hearing various cases, complaints and grievances of their members. Those of us who have to pronounce judgement on person and situations are to view the exercise of our authority as a service of the truth for the common good as well as for the well-being of the individual. In particular, we exhort the people of God to respect the right of defence of those accused of having committed offences.

CONCLUSION

The issues raised in this letter will obviously require an ongoing and in-depth reflection. It is the Church's mission to preach the Gospel which effects the redemption of the human race and its liberation from every oppressive situation, be it hunger, ignorance, blindness, despair, paralysing fear, etc. Like Jesus, the advocates of the poor and the oppressed, the believing community is invited, at times obliged in justice, to show in action a preferential love for the economically disadvantaged, the voiceless who live in situations of hopelessness.

The human rights and duties identified in this pastoral letter for our reflection are only some of the issues that our God invites us to consider seriously. In our response to God, we humbly recognise that though a gifted and blessed people, we are not a perfect community. If some of our personal weaknesses, biases and ambitions are not purified by the word of God and just laws, they can very easily destroy peace and harmony in our societies and communities. We hope that our message will deepen in all of us the experience of conversion and the desire for the truth and the light of Christ. This will prepare us for the worthy celebration of Easter, the feast of the risen Lord in whom we see ourselves as a risen people with dignity restored.

Archbishop J. Chiona
Bishop F. Mikhori
Bishop M. A. Chimole
Bishop A. Assolari
Bishop A. Chamgwera
Bishop G. M. Chisendera
Monsignor J. Roche